English Language Learners

Vocabulary Building Games & Activities

Songs, Storytelling, Rhymes, Chants, Picture Books,
Games, and Reproducible Activities That Promote
Natural and Purposeful Communication in Young Children

by
Sherrill B. Flora

illustrations by
Timothy Irwin

Publisher
Key Education Publishing Company, LLC
Minneapolis, Minnesota 55431

www.keyeducationpublishing.com

CONGRATULATIONS ON YOUR PURCHASE OF A KEY EDUCATION PRODUCT!

The editors at Key Education are former teachers who bring experience, enthusiasm, and quality to each and every product. Thousands of teachers have looked to the staff at Key Education for new and innovative resources to make their work more enjoyable and rewarding. Key Education is committed to developing and publishing educational materials that will assist teachers in building a strong and developmentally appropriate curriculum for young children.

PLAN FOR GREAT TEACHING EXPERIENCES WHEN YOU USE
EDUCATIONAL MATERIALS FROM KEY EDUCATION PUBLISHING COMPANY, LLC

Credits
Author: Sherrill B. Flora
Creative Director: Annette Hollister-Papp
Cover Design: Annette Hollister-Papp
Illustrator: Timothy Irwin
Editors: Karen Seberg and Claude Chalk
Production: Key Education Staff

Key Education welcomes manuscripts and product ideas from teachers. For a copy of our submission guidelines, please send a self-addressed, stamped envelope to:
Key Education Publishing Company, LLC
Acquisitions Department
9601 Newton Avenue South
Minneapolis, Minnesota 55431

Original Music in Chapter 6: Thematic Units was written by Kathryn Wheeler

Note to Teacher: To hear the tunes that go with these lyrics, or to find the original lyrics for each song, go to the National Institute of Health Department site for children's music at the Department of Health and Human Services web site: http://kids.niehs.nih.gov/musicchild.htm.

Special Note
Before completing any balloon activity, ask families about latex allergies. Also, remember that uninflated or popped balloons may present a choking hazard.

Standard Book Number: 978-1-602680-51-7
English Language Learners: Vocabulary Building Games & Activities
Copyright © 2009 by Key Education Publishing Company, LLC
Minneapolis, Minnesota 55431

Introduction

Over the years, reading research has accumulated a wealth of evidence identifying the strong relationship between the extent of students' vocabulary knowledge and the ability to comprehend what they have read, as well as their overall academic success. The National Reading Panel (2000) has written that direct instruction for vocabulary development is important for all students, but it is **crucial** for English language learners (ELL) and for students who are at risk for learning how to read. The National Reading Panel also wrote that dependence on a single vocabulary instructional method will not result in optimal learning and that the use of a variety of methods is more effective.

English Language Learners: Vocabulary Building Games & Activities offers teachers hundreds of ideas to create learning environments that are filled with rich oral language and encourage children's active engagement. A variety of instructional methods can be found in this book including selecting vocabulary; effectively using children's literature; reading aloud; applying Teaching Proficiency through Reading and Storytelling (TPRS) and Total Physical Response (TPR); employing songs, rhymes, chants, and musical activities to help children imitate and remember language; and utilizing games as valuable teaching tools.

Research has shown that "playing games" is a natural and effective method for teaching and practicing vocabulary, increasing fluency, introducing new concepts and ideas, and applying language within a meaningful context. Engaging in such play can be motivational for children while decreasing their frustration and anxiety levels.

English Language Learners: Vocabulary Building Games & Activities will help classroom teachers develop strategies, activities, and interventions that can be used throughout the day to make learning fun, promote receptive and expressive language, and help children achieve academic success.

Contents

Chapter 6: THEMATIC UNITS

Chapter 1: Guide for Educators

The United States is currently experiencing rapid growth in linguistic and cultural diversity; this growth can easily be seen within the public schools. This increase in diversity is also creating classrooms with growing numbers of children whose native language is not English, described as English language learners (ELL) or limited English proficient (LEP). The availability of special instructional programs for ELL students, such as bilingual education, English as a Second Language (ESL), and English for Speakers of Other Languages (ESOL) differs greatly across the country. These types of programs may be provided through mainstream classes or a self-contained language class or a child may be pulled out for special one-to-one tutoring or speech and language instruction.

The No Child Left Behind Act as well as other local, state, and federal school reform programs necessitate increased school accountability for all students, including English language learners. Providing the best possible education for children learning English has become the responsibility of all educators. English language learners are found in every state across the country, with the largest ELL populations in Arizona, California, Florida, New York, and Texas.

The classroom teacher's job of teaching becomes more manageable and more effective when the teacher gains an understanding of some of the unique challenges faced by young English language learners; is able to learn about each student's life and cultural experiences; develops a knowledge of second language acquisition; and establishes some strategies and interventions that can be utilized throughout the day to promote language development and school success.

Second Language Acquisition

Basic Interpersonal Communication Skills (BICS) and Cognitive Academic Language Proficiency (CALP)

It is important for teachers to understand that children acquire language on two different developmental levels as described by language acquisition expert Jim Cummins. The first level is basic interpersonal communication skills (BICS). **BICS is social language**—the language needed for everyday communication. For example, ELLs use BICS when playing, talking in the hallways at school, or eating lunch together. Social language skills usually develop in a student's first six months to two years in the United States.

Sometimes when young children have developed good social language, they can give the impression of being proficient in speaking English but may not actually have enough English language to be academically successful. This leads to the next developmental level, which is cognitive academic language proficiency (CALP). **CALP is the language needed for academic learning**—including listening, speaking, reading, and writing about content material in various subject areas. CALP usually takes from five to seven years to develop. Current research shows that children who have not been to school or who have not had any support in their native language development may actually need from seven to ten years to catch up academically with their peers.

Stages of Second Language Acquisition

The following are the first four stages of second language acquisition as developed by linguist Stephen Krashen. It is important to know which stage each of your ELLs is in and to remember that the length of time spent at each phase may vary greatly from one child to the next.

Stage I: Preproduction (The Silent Stage, including Observation, Imitation, and Gestures)

This is the **silent stage** where children are listening and trying to make sense of what is going on around them. Although some of these children may have developed a receptive vocabulary of up to 500 words, they are not yet verbalizing.

Some young English language learners will repeat everything they hear. These children may **imitate** the words spoken to them, nod yes and no, or draw and point. These children are interested in language and may be good at imitation, but they are not actually producing "real" language.

In this silent phase, teachers should use strategies that include simplified speech, gestures, pointing, acting out, frequent repetition, props, visuals, modeling, and demonstrating. Total Physical Response (TPR) methods also work well with children demonstrating the preproduction stage of language behaviors.

Stage 2: Early Production (Single Words and Phrases)

Children may be in this stage up to six months and develop a receptive and expressive vocabulary of about 1,000 words. These words usually consist of short sentences such as, "That's mine," "Come here," "Sit down," and yes and no responses. It is important to remember that when children are first learning a new language, they will understand much more than they are able to verbalize.

Here are some suggestions for encouraging language development for children in this phase:

- ❖ Ask yes or no questions.
- ❖ Encourage one or two word answers.
- ❖ Use realistic photographs and pictures to build vocabulary.
- ❖ Offer listening activities.
- ❖ Share picture books with predictable text.
- ❖ Use graphic organizers, charts, and graphs.
- ❖ Create a print-rich environment with many classroom labels.

Stage 3: Speech Emergence (Beginning to Understand Grammatical Rules)

Students in this stage may have developed a vocabulary of 3,000 words. They can communicate with simple phrases and short sentences of three to four words, which may contain errors in grammar or pronunciation. They are also beginning to ask simple questions and initiate conversations with friends.

Here are some suggestions to encourage further language development:

- ❖ Support short, modified texts in content area subjects with illustrations or photographs.
- ❖ Provide word banks to use with graphic organizers.
- ❖ Use vocabulary flash cards for content areas.
- ❖ Incorporate choral reading and readers' theater activities.
- ❖ Encourage children to work in pairs and small groups with hands-on activities.

Stage 4: Intermediate Fluency

Students at the intermediate fluency stage have a vocabulary of 6,000 active words and can use these words to speak in more complex sentences. They are able to state opinions, ask detailed questions, and share their own thoughts. Their social language skills are excellent, but they may still experience difficulties with the more cognitively demanding subjects when a high degree of literacy is required, such as social studies and English. ELLs at this level may be able complete math and science activities at grade level with minimal teacher support.

In this stage, students have excellent comprehension and are able to understand more complex concepts. However, their writing may contain many errors as they work to master English grammar and sentence structure. Students should be able to synthesize and to make inferences about what they are learning.

Activities to encourage further language development are brainstorming, clustering, categorizing, charting, journal or log writing, and reading and writing to acquire relevant information.

Selecting Vocabulary

Words are the building blocks of language. The more vocabulary words children acquire, the faster they will be able to use their new language for meaningful communication.

First Words

Young children are able to learn new vocabulary words quickly when new words are presented in concrete terms—meaning words that children can **see**, **touch**, **taste**, **hear**, and **play with**. For example, it is easy to teach the word *cookie* when children experience baking cookies and then have the fun of eating cookies. It is also easy to teach a word like *jump* or *walk* because the meaning of the word can be demonstrated. Providing children with a bank of vocabulary words to draw upon is crucial, so begin with survival vocabulary—words that newcomers or preproduction beginners really need to know, such as:

- name, address, and phone number
- social greetings, such as "Hello" or "How are you?"
- classroom and school survival words (pencil, bathroom, etc.)
- clothing
- body parts
- everyday objects (cup, pillow, etc.)
- words for naming family and friends
- numbers, calendar, and time
- animals

Key Vocabulary Words

When teaching new vocabulary to young ELL students it is important to select key vocabulary for each unit or lesson you will be teaching. For example, the story of "The Three Little Pigs" would have very little meaning to ELL students if they did not understand the key vocabulary words *pig, wolf, bricks, sticks,* and *straw.* These key words should be taught before the story is introduced and read to the class.

Here are some questions that teachers should ask themselves when selecting key vocabulary:
- Which words in the unit are essential to know?
- Which words are important to know?
- Which words are nice to know?

ELLs should be immersed in the key words. Here are some ideas for how you can teach and display new key words:
- Pronounce the word and provide a concrete definition (i.e., show a photo or an object, act it out, or provide a hands-on activity).
- Create word walls of key words and display pictures of the definition for reference.
- Generate and record sentences containing the words building on original or familiar context.
- Use the word often in instruction and point out the word in other content areas.
- Have students find and use the word.
- Add the word to a classroom word bank or to student-made dictionaries.
- Use the student's first language to clarify the word's meaning.
- Create word webs.
- Invite students to act out the word, using visuals or real objects (realia).

Tips for Supporting
Young English Language Learners

Learn about Culture and Family

❖ Ask each child's name and learn how to pronounce it correctly.

❖ Learn as much as possible about the cultural backgrounds and languages of the ELL students in your classroom.

❖ Use culturally relevant materials to enhance children's self-images, motivation, and cultural pride. Encourage activities that highlight the children's cultures.

❖ Invite parents to become actively involved in their child's education. If they do not respond to notes sent home, call the family or request social workers to make home visits. Try to communicate with parents in their native language whenever possible. You may need to enlist the aid of interpreters or bilingual school staff.

Your Expectations

❖ Set high expectations and prepare children to meet state and national academic standards. It is always better to set high goals rather than not expecting enough.

❖ Clearly state the rules and expected behaviors of your classroom. Children feel more secure when they understand rules and know what is expected of them

❖ Seek help from other professionals when you need it. School psychologists, social workers, and counselors can offer you support that will help create the best environment for your English language learners.

Classroom Modifications and Materials

❖ Teach survival English vocabulary first, for example, *lunchroom*, *bathroom*, *pencil*, and so on. Write labels in English for objects in the classroom.

❖ Directions in English should be brief and clear. Avoid jargon that will not be understood.

❖ At first, the frequent repetition of directions may be needed. Observe to see if students really understand what they are expected to do.

❖ Instruction should be at the same level as your ELLs' language proficiency skills and current functioning. This may require aligning curriculum, assessment, and interventions to meet their needs.

❖ Provide instructional support in the students' native languages while they are learning English.

❖ Match a new ELL student with a bilingual student who can speak the student's language and act as a buddy.

❖ Foster communication in the classroom that is natural and purposeful. Give children plenty of practice in listening and speaking and eventually with reading and writing.

❖ Use a variety of teaching aids and technologies to reinforce learning, such as computers, tape recorders, language masters, and overhead projectors as well as hands-on objects and experiences such as games, photographs, music, and art.

❖ Encourage students' participation in extracurricular activities.

❖ Motivate the development of talents, hobbies, and special interests.

❖ Make use of many types of active and interactive learning, including cooperative learning groups, role-playing, dialogue journals, choral chants, and readers' theater.

❖ Locate sources for—and then share with families—homework support activities or hotlines staffed by bilingual teachers, aides, and volunteers.

❖ Obtain and teach students to use dictionaries that contain translations from the children's native languages to English and vice versa.

❖ Combine nonverbal gestures and visuals with oral communication, especially when introducing new material.

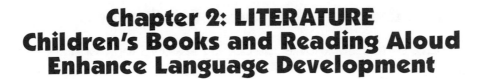

Chapter 2: LITERATURE
Children's Books and Reading Aloud
Enhance Language Development

Literature is a powerful and motivational educational resource that can enrich language development in young English language learners. When teachers read aloud children's books or tell stories (using any number of storytelling techniques), they are modeling literacy skills, cultivating listening skills, and are promoting natural vocabulary acquisition in children.

Literature is obviously an essential tool for language arts instruction, but it is also an effective teaching tool for many learning areas, such as the following:

❖ Literature is a great way for ELLs to share information about their own cultures and learn about the different cultures of their classmates.

❖ Literature incorporated into other subject areas, such as math or science, often helps ELLs understand new content.

❖ Presenting a variety of types of literature can increase a desire to read.

❖ Since literature is authentic, vocabulary and grammar are promoted naturally as children listen to, and learn from, each story.

❖ Children who are provided the opportunity to listen to and learn from a wide variety of stories may also demonstrate increased oral and written language skills.

Choosing Children's Books: Teacher Preparation

❖ **Choose stories that meet the interests and experiences of your students.** It is best to begin with stories that are humorous and represent topics your students are familiar with. If students already have some knowledge of the content, this will help them connect any new words with the meaning of the text. (See the Recommended Read Aloud Book List on pages 13 and 14.)

❖ **Find great illustrations or photographs.** For young ELLs, choose books with wonderful illustrations or photographs. Good visual clues will help children grasp more meaning.

❖ **Provide predictable and repetitive content.** Young ELLs benefit from stories that have a high degree of repetition and have predictable content.

❖ **Spend time learning the story yourself.** Know the story well so that you can prepare students for the new vocabulary used throughout the story, such as action words and names of objects and story characters.

❖ **Plan enough time for sharing the story.** A well-prepared and presented story can enchant children. Make sure you have allowed enough time for children to respond, ask questions, and experiment with using new vocabulary.

Before You Share the Story: Preparing ELL Students

Young ELLs must have some prior knowledge about the story's topic and concepts and recognize the key vocabulary in order to understand the meaning of the story. Take time to assess students' background knowledge and the key vocabulary words that will need to be pretaught. The following are some ideas to assist you in preteaching key vocabulary and new concepts:

❖ **Employ hands-on experiences to present new words and concepts.** For example, make and eat popcorn if the story is about popcorn. If the story is about bugs, first collect some bugs to observe and then release them.

❖ **Use real objects and real photographs as much as possible.** This is good not only for objects (nouns), but can also be used to teach concepts. Children may understand a concept such as racing but not have the words *race, raced,* or *racing* in their vocabularies.

❖ **Invite children to create illustrations.** New vocabulary and concepts will be reinforced when children draw pictures of characters, places, and objects from the story before the story is shared.

❖ **Examine the cover of the book with the children.** Tell children the title of the story, as well as the names of the author and illustrator. Talk about the illustration on the cover and give a brief overview of what the story will be about (without giving away surprises or important story details). Start a simple informative discussion such as, "This is a story about a turtle and a rabbit. How does a turtle move? How does a rabbit move?" Encourage children to try to predict what might happen in the story.

While You Are Sharing the Story: Making the Most of Language

❖ **Use storytelling props.** Commercially made puppets, teacher-made stick puppets, and flannel or magnetic board characters that can be manipulated as the story is told are additional ways for children to "see" the story and gain meaning.

❖ **Dramatize word meanings with gestures, body movements, and facial expressions.** Gestures, body movements, and facial expressions can instantly relate the meaning of a word or phrase. For example, quickly show the content of the sentence, "She was scared and dove under her blankets," by showing fear on your face and then pretending to cover yourself with a blanket. Never be shy! Dramatizing provides meaning and is very entertaining for young children. (See Total Physical Response and Teaching Proficiency through Reading and Storytelling on page 12.)

❖ **Print word cards and predicable text cards.** Even if children are not yet reading, make word cards for new vocabulary. Eventually children will associate the printed text with spoken words. Predictable text cards are also great fun to use when telling a story. For example, in the story "Jack and the Beanstalk," make one card for "Fe, fi, fo fum, I spell the blood of an Englishman." Each time the giant appears, hold up the predictable text card and have children pretend to be the giant as they repeat the chant.

❖ **Examine the illustrations.** Be sure to provide children with enough time to examine the story's illustrations. Especially for young children, illustrations are often the key to understanding a story. Don't rush. Point out interesting aspects in each illustration. Encourage children to look for specific details and indicate things that are of special interest to them.

- **Examine the text while you read.** Point out words that rhyme or have alliteration and encourage children to think of additional rhyming words or more words with the same beginning sounds.

- **Watch out for boredom.** Even if you have prepared well, there may be times when young children become bored. Do not let the story become tiresome. If children look disengaged, read with more excitement or even put the story away to be continued another day. You may simply need to choose another book—not every story will be a success.

- **Observe the children for confusion.** Puzzled children will not be good listeners. Young ELLs may appear to understand more receptive language than they really do. If your students look confused, please stop and clarify. Discover what has not been understood.

- **Make predictions and draw conclusions.** Have children share their predictions about what will happen in the story. Then, as you are reading and the story is unfolding, point out to students which predictions were correct. Ask if there were any surprises instead of what they thought would happen. What conclusions can students draw?

When the Story Is Finished: Extending Language

- **Discuss reactions to the story.** At the end of the story encourage children to express what they liked or disliked about the story. What were some of their favorite parts? Who were their favorite characters? Why? Is there anything about the story that they would change? Then, share some of your own thoughts about the story.

- **Act out the story.** Using a shorter version if necessary, let children have the fun of acting out the story as you reread it.

- **Sequence the illustrations.** For educational purposes, copy (or create your own) illustrations from the story. Hand out the illustrations and have children put the pictures in the correct story sequence.

- **Create your own classroom big book.** Divide children into small cooperative learning groups. Give each group a piece of poster board and crayons and assign a scene from the story for the group to illustrate. When the groups' drawings are finished, put the pages in the correct sequence and bind them together with yarn. Children will enjoy looking at their own big books and naming things in the story—or they may even try to retell the story's events.

- **Plan a story show-and-tell.** Ask children to bring something from home that relates to the story. Invite students to share their objects and the story connection.

- **Make a bulletin board of favorite classroom stories.** Each time you read a story, attach a picture of the cover to a bulletin board. Children can use this as a reference when selecting stories to hear again. This is also a fun way to reinforce vocabulary that has already been taught. For example, if you have already read the story "The Three Little Pigs," the cover will be displayed on the bulletin board. Then, when you read a story about farms, you can point out that students have already learned about pigs and now will learn about other farm animals. Or, you might ask, "Do you think the three pigs would have liked to live on a farm?" Link the elements of different stories whenever possible.

- **Connect, connect, connect.** Remember, when you are finished with the story, the goal of the postreading activities is to connect the key vocabulary with new concepts to increase comprehension.

Total Physical Response (TPR) and Teaching Proficiency through Reading and Storytelling (TPRS)

What is Total Physical Response (TPR)?

Total Physical Response (TPR) is a method designed to help people learn a foreign language. It was developed in the late 1960s by Dr. James J. Asher, a professor of psychology at San José State University in California. TPR is based on observing how infants learn language and the premise that the human brain has a biological program for acquiring language. Parents and infants first communicate with each other with a parent's speech and physical touches and responses. For many months, infants absorb language but are not able to talk. Eventually, when the child has decoded enough of the language, speech is produced spontaneously. TPR in the classroom tries to replicate this process with students responding physically to the words of the teacher. For example, playing the game Simon Says is a TPR activity.

What is Teaching Proficiency through Reading and Storytelling (TPRS)?

Blaine Ray, a Spanish teacher, realized that TPR was limited when teaching abstract language concepts. In the 1990s, he developed an additional method of TPR called Teaching Proficiency through Reading and Storytelling (TPRS). Simply explained, teachers tell a story while asking many questions in the language children are learning, and the children contribute to and act out the story.

TPRS begins with introducing and personalizing the vocabulary. Students then apply the targeted vocabulary to the story by performing after each statement. The teacher tells, retells, and asks questions about the story. Finally, the oral story is followed up with written text. The holistic approach of TPRS helps students to rapidly acquire the second language.

Books with TPR elements:

- Brown, Marcia. *Sopa de Piedras/Stone Soup.* Alladin, 2005.
- Carle, Eric. *La oruga muy hambrienta/The Very Hungry Caterpillar.* Philomel, 1986.
- Ginsburg, Mirra. *The Chick and the Duckling.* Houghton Mifflin, 1998.
- González, Lucia. *The Bossy Gallito.* Scholastic, 1999.
- Guarino, Deborah. *Is Your Mama a Llama?* Scholastic, 2004.
- Marshall, James. *Goldilocks and the Three Bears.* Puffin Books, 1998.
- Masurel, Claire. *Diez Perros en la Tienda.* Night Sky Books, 2000.
- Rosa-Casanova, Sylvia. *Mama Provi and the Pot of Rice.* Atheneum, 1997.
- Rosen, Michael. *We're Going on a Bear Hunt/Vamos a cazar un oso.* Alladin, 2003.
- Slobodkina, Esphyr. *Caps for Sale.* HarperTrophy, 1996.
- Taback, Simms. *There Was an Old Lady Who Swallowed a Fly.* Child's Play international, 2003.
- Tolstoy, Alexei. *The Great Big Enormous Turnip.* Mammoth, 1998.
- Walsh, Ellen Stoll. *Mouse Count/Cuenta ratones.* Voyager Books, 1995.
- Wood, Audrey. *The Napping House.* Harcourt Children's Books, 2004.

RECOMMENDED READ ALOUD BOOK LIST

Alphabet
- Aylesworth, Jim. *Old Black Fly*. Henry Holt and Co. 1995.
- Carlson, Nancy. *ABC I Like Me*. Viking. 1997
- Ehlert, Lois. *Eating the Alphabet: Fruits & Vegetables from A to Z*. Harcourt Big Books. 1994.
- Dr. Seuss. *Dr. Seuss's ABC: An Amazing Alphabet Book!* Random House Books. 1996
- Gerstein, Mordicai. *The Awful Alphabet Book*. Voyager Books, 2001.

Animals
- Brown, Demi. *Touch and Feel Wild Animals*. Dorling Kindersley Publishing. 1998.
- Barton, Byron. *The Three Bears*. HarperCollins, 1991.
- Burton, Marilee Robin. *Tails Toes Eyes Ears Nose*. HarperCollins.1988.
- Campbell, Rod. *Dear Zoo*. Campbell Books. 2007.
- Emberly, Rebecca. *My Animals/Mis animales*. Little, Brown & Company. Bilingual Edition: English & Spanish 2002.
- Ehlert, Lois. *Nuts to You!* Voyager Books. 2004.
- Feiffer, Jules et all. *Muncha! Muncha! Muncha!* Simon & Schuster, 2003.
- Fleming, Denise. *In the Tall, Tall Grass*. Henry Holt and Co. 1995.
- Fleming, Denise. *In the Small, Small Pond*. Henry Holt and Co. 2007.
- Gollub, Matthew. *The Jazz Fly*. Tortuga Press. 2000.
- Martin Jr., Bill and Carle, Eric. *Panda Bear, Panda Bear, What Do You See?* Henry Holt and Company, LLC.2003.
- McCloskey, Robert. *Make Way for Ducklings*. Penguin Group. 1941.
- Paterson, Betina. *My First Wild Animals*. HarperCollins. 1991.
- Wiesner, David. *The Three Pigs*. Clarion Books. 2001.

Body Parts
- Carle, Eric. *From Head to Toe*. Harper Festival. Board Edition 1999.
- Hester, Elizabeth. *All About Me* (DK Lift-the-Flap Book). Dorling Kindersley Publishing. 2003.
- Katz, Karen. *Where Is Baby's Belly Button?* Little Simon. 2000.

Clothing
- Emberly, Rebecca. *My Clothes/Mi ropa*. Little, Brown & Company. Bilingual Edition: English & Spanish. 2002.
- Estes, Eleanor. *The Hundred Dresses*. Harcourt. 2004.
- Fung, Karen. *Zipper, Buttons and Bows*. Barron's Educational Series, Inc. 2000.
- Katz, Karen. *Toes, Ears, and Nose!* A Lift-the-Flap Book. Little Simon. 2003.

Colors
- Carle, Eric. *Grouchy Ladybug*. HarperCollins Children's Books. 1977.
- Cote, Pamela. *What Color Is It?/¿Qué color es éste?*. Houghton Mifflin Company. 2002.
- Ehlert, Lois. *Color Farm*. HarperCollins. 1990.
- Ehlert, Lois. *Color Zoo*. HarperCollins. 1989.
- Ehlert, Lois. *Planting a Rainbow*. Harcourt. 1992.
- Emberley, Rebecca. *My Colors/Mis colores*. Little, Brown & Company. 2000.
- Graves, Kimberlee. *Colors of My Day*. Rebound by Sagebrush. 1997.
- Hoban, Tana. *Of Colors and Things*. HarperTrophy. 1st Mulberry Edition 1996.
- Lionni, Leo. *Color of His Own*. Bantam Doubleday Dell Books for Young Readers. 1997.
- Martin, Bill Jr. and Carle, Eric. *Brown Bear, Brown Bear, What Do You See?* Henry Holt and Company, Inc. 1996.
- Walsh, Ellen Stoll. *Mouse Paint*. Red Wagon Books. 1995.

Community Helpers
- Caseley, Judith. *On the Town: A Community Adventure*. Greenwillow Press. 2002.
- Cousins, Lucy. *Maisy Drives the Bus*. Candlewick Press. 2000.
- Ernst, Lisa. *The Letters Are Lost!* Puffin, 1999.
- Kalmar, Bobbie and Walker, Niki. *Community Helpers from A to Z* (Alphabasics). Crabtree Publishing Company. 1997.
- Kalmon, Bobbie, Walker, Nikki. *Community Helpers from A to Z*. Crabtree Publishing Company. 1997.
- Kottke, Jan. *A Day with a Mail Carrier*. Children's Press. 2000.
- Liebman, Dan. *I Want to Be a Firefighter* . Firefly Books LTD. 1999.
- Maynard, Christopher. *Jobs People Do*. DK Publishing, Inc. 2001.
- Rathman, Peggy. *Officer Buckle and Gloria*. Putnam Publishing Group.1995.
- Rockwell, Anne. *Career Day*. HarperCollins. 2000.

Emotions
- Bang, Molly. *When Sophie Gets Angry—Really, Really Angry...* . (Caldecott Honor Book). Scholastic. 1999.
- Boynton, Sandra. *A is for Angry*. Workman Publishing. 1987.
- Burningham, John. *Mr. Grumpy's Outing*. Henry Holt and Co. 1970.
- Cain, Janan. *The Way I Feel*. Parenting Press. 2000.
- Crary, Elizabeth, et al. *When You're Happy: And You Know It*. Parenting Press. 1996.
- Crary, Elizabeth, et al. *When You're Mad: And You Know It*. Parenting Press. 1996.
- Curtis, Jamie Lee and Cornell, Laura. *It's Hard to Be Five: Learning How to Work My Control Panels*. Joanna Colter. 2004.
- Curtis, Jamie Lee and Cornell, Laura. *Today I Feel Silly: And Other Moods That Make My Day*. Joanna Colter. 1998.
- Emberly, Rebecca. *How Do I Feel?/¿Cómo me siento?* Houghton Mifflin. 2002.
- Litchenheld, Tom. *What Are You So Grumpy About?* Little, Brown & Company. 2003.

Everyday Objects
- Amery, Heather and Cartwright, Stephen. *The Usborne First Thousand Words*. Usborne Books. 2003.
- Arnold, Tedd. *No More Water in the Tub!* Puffin Books. 1998.
- Conrad, Pam. *The Tub People*. HarperTrophy. 1st Harper Edition. 1995.
- Crowther, Robert. *Robert Crowther's Amazing Pop-Up House of Inventions & Hundreds of Fabulous Facts About Where You Live*. Candlewick Press. 2000.
- Gorner, Terri. *1001 Things to Spot in the Town*. E.D.C. Publishing. 2001.
- Litchfield, Jo, et all. *The Usborne Book of Everyday Words*. E.D.C. Publishing. 1999.
- Rex, Michael. *Pie is Cherry (Kitchen Things)*. Henry Holt & Company. 2001.

Family/Friends
- Aliki. *We Are Best Friends*. HarperTrophy. 1987.
- Berhard, Emery. *A Ride on Mother's Back: A Day of Carrying Baby Around the World*. Gulliver Books. 1996.
- Bridwell, Norman. *Clifford's Family*. Scholastic. 1984.
- Gordon, Sol, Cohen, Vivian. *All Families Are Different*. Prometheus Books. 2000.
- Flournoy, Valerie. *The Patchwork Quilt*. Dial Books. 1985.
- Fox, Mem. *Where Is the Green Sheep?* Harcourt Children's Books. 2004.
- Johnson, Angela and Soman, David. *Daddy Calls Me Man*. Orchard Books. © 2000.
- Johnson, Angela and Soman, David. *Tell Me a Story, Mama*. Orchard Books. 1989.
- Johnson, Angela and Soman, David. *When I Am Old With You*. Franklin Watts, Inc. 1993.

- Lenski, Lois. *The Little Family*. Random House Books for Young Readers. 2002.
- Levinson, Riki. *I Go with My Family to Grandma's*. Puffin Books. 1986.
- Long, Earlene. *Gone Fishing*. Houghton Mifflin. 1984.
- Parr, Todd. *The Family Book*. Megan Tingley. 2003.
- Rotner, Shelley and Kelly, Sheila. *Lots of Moms*. Dial. 1996.
- Rylant, Cynthia. *The Relatives Came*. Alladin. 1993.
- Skutch, Robert, Nienhaus, Laura. *Who's in Your Family?* Tricycle Press. 1997.
- Wallner, Alexandra. *Farmer in the Dell*. Holiday House. 1998.

Food

- Buono, Anthony and Nemerson, Roy. *The Race Against Junk Food*. HCom. 1997.
- Ehlert, Lois. Eating the Alphabet: *Fruits and Vegetables from A to Z*. Harcourt Children's Books. 1989.
- Ehlert, Lois. *Growing Vegetable Soup*. Voyager Books. 1990.
- Emberly, Rebecca. *My Foods/Mi comida*. Little, Brown & Company. Bilingual Edition: English & Spanish. 2002.
- Fleming, Denise. *Lunch*. Henry Holt and Company. 1998.
- Leedy, Loreen. *The Edible Pyramid*. Holiday House. 1996.
- Sears, Martha and Sears, William and Kelly, Christie Watts. *Eat Healthy, Feel Great*. Little, Brown. 2002.
- Sharmat, Mitchell. *Gregory, the Terrible Eater*. Scholastic. 1985.

Manners

- Berenstain, Stan and Jan. *The Berenstain Bears and the Truth*. Random House.1983.
- Bridwell, Norman. *Clifford's Manners*. Scholastic. 1987.
- Cole, Joanna. *Sharing is Fun*. HarperCollins. 2004.
- Katz, Karen. *Excuse Me!: A Little Book of Manners*. Grosset & Dunlap. 2002.
- Meiners, Cheri. *Share and Take Turns (Learning to Get Along)*. Free Spirit Publishing. 2003.

Numbers

- Christelow, Eileen. *Five Little Monkeys Jumping on the Bed*. Clarion Books. 1998.
- Crews, Donald. *Ten Black Dots*. HarperTrophy. 1995.
- Ernst, Lisa Campbell. *Up to Ten and Down Again*. Lothrop, Lee & Shephard Books. 1986.
- Hamm, Diane Johnston. *How Many Feet in Bed?* Aladdin. 1991.
- Hoban, Tana. *Count and See*. Simon & Schuster Children's Publishing. 1972.
- Hutchins, Pat. *1 Hunter*. HarperTrophy. 1982.
- Mitsumasa, Anno. *Anno's Counting Book*. HarperTrophy. 1976.
- Sloat, Terri. *From One to One Hundred*. Puffin Books. 1991.
- Walsh, Ellen Stoll. *Mouse Counts*. Red Wagon Books. 1995.

Opposites

- Bridwell, Norman. *Clifford's Opposites*. Scholastic, Inc. 2000.
- Burningham, John. *Opposites*. Candlewick Press. 2003.
- Falconer, Ian. *Olivia's Opposites*. Simon & Schuster Children's Books. 2002.
- Fox, Mem. *Where Is the Green Sheep?* Harcourt. 2004.
- Hoban, Tana. *Exactly the Opposites*. William Morrow & Company, Inc. 1997.
- Huelin, Jodi. *Harold and the Purple Crayon: Opposites*. HarperCollins Children's Books. 2004.
- Patricelli, Leslie. *Yummy Yucky*. Candlewick Press. 2003.
- Seuss, Dr. *One Fish, Two Fish, Red Fish, Blue Fish*. Random House, Inc. 1976.
- Seuss, Dr. *The Foot Book: Dr. Seuss's Wacky Book of Opposites*. Random House, Inc. 1996.

School

- Danneberg, Julie and Love, Judith DuFour. *First Day Jitters*. Charlesbridge Publishing, Inc. 2000.

- Kids Can Press, Ltd. *Franklin Goes to School*. Scholastic, Inc. 1995.
- Murkoff Heidi. *What to Expect at Preschool* HarperFestival, 2001.
- Slate, Joseph, Wolff, Ashley. *Miss Bindergarten Gets Ready for Kindergarten*. Puffin Books, 1996.
- Numeroff, Laura. *If You Take A Mouse to School*. Laura Geringer Books. 2002.
- Snyder, Inez. *School Tools*. Scholastic Library Publishing. 2001.
- Weiss, Ellen and Weiss, Leatie. *My Teacher Sleeps in School*. Puffin Books. 1985.
- Wiseman, B. *Morris Goes to School*. HarperCollins Publishers. 1983.

Verbs/Actions

- Arnold, Tedd. *No Jumping on the Bed!* Puffin. 1996.
- Baer, Edith. *This is the Way We Go to School*. Scholastic, Inc. 1990.
- Burningham, John. *Would You Rather....* Chronicle Books. 2003.
- Caseley, Judith. *Field Day Friday*. Greenwillow. 2000.
- Dunn, Opal. *Acka Backa Boo!: Playground Games from Around the World*. Henry Holt & Company, Inc. 2000.
- Falconer, Ian. *Olivia*. Simon & Schuster Children's Publishing. 2000.
- Gollub, Matthew. *The Jazz Fly*. Tortuga Press. 2000.
- Lionni, Leo. *Let's Play*. Knoph Books for Young Readers. 2003.
- Yolen, Jane. *How Do Dinosaurs Clean Their Rooms*. Scholastic, Inc. 2004.
- Berger, Terry et all. *Ben's ABC Day*. William Morrow & Company Library. 1982.
- Gundersheim, Karen. *ABC, Say with Me*. HarperCollins Publishers.1984.
- Hood, Christine. *Just Like Me (Learn to Read, Read to Learn)*. Rebound by Sagebrush. 1996.
- Kent, Jack. *Jack Kent's Hop, Skip, and Jump Book: An Action Word Book*. Random House. 1974.
- Maestro, Betsy. *Busy Book of Action Words*. Random House Value Publishing. 1988.
- Noll, Sally. *Jiggle, Wiggle, Prance*. Puffin Books. Reprint Edition. 1993.

Toys

- Cronin, Doreen. *Diary of a Worm*. HarperCollins Publishers. 2003.
- Falconer, Ian. *Olivia . . . and the Missing Toy*. Simon & Schuster Children's Publishing. 2003.
- Freeman, Don. *Corduroy*. Puffin Books. Reprinted Edition. 1968.
- Murphy, Stuart J. *Beep Beep, Vroom Vroom!* HarperCollins Children's Books. 1999.
- Piekart, Ferry. *Playing with Stuff: Outrageous Games with Ordinary Objects*. Kane/Miller Book Publishers. 2004.

Transportation

- Barton, Byron. *Airport*. Harper Trophy. 1987.
- Burton, Virginia Lee. *Choo-Choo*. Houghton Mifflin.1988.
- Kate McMullan. *I Stink!* Joanna Cotler. 2002.
- Watty Piper, George Hauman, Doris Hauman. *The Little Engine that Could*. Penguin Books for Young Readers. 1978.
- H.A. Rey. *Curious George and the Dump Truck*. Houghton Mifflin. 1999.

Weather

- Hall, Zoe. *Fall Leaves Fall!* Scholastic Press. 2000.
- Hutchins, Pat. *The Wind Blew*. Alladin. 1993.
- Kaplan, Robert. *Rain*. HarperTrophy. 1991.
- Karen Pandell, Tomie de Paola. *I Love You Sun, I Love You Moon*. Putnam Juvenile. 2003.

Chapter 3: MUSIC
The Importance of Songs, Rhymes, Chants, and Musical Activities

Songs, rhymes, chants, and musical activities provide wonderful language learning experiences for young ELLs. Music is fun for young children, authentic, comprehensible, and full of language. Music has been shown to be so successful for second language acquisition that it is now common practice to use songs and music in the classroom to teach many concepts. For example, use music to teach basic vocabulary, including colors, body parts, simple actions and phrases, clothes, and names of people and animals. And remember, a teacher does not have to be musically talented to effectively use music in the classroom. Here are just a few reasons why the use of music benefits second language learning:

- ❖ Singing words, rather than speaking them, makes it easier for children to imitate and remember language.

- ❖ Singing helps children acquire a sense of rhythm.

- ❖ Songs, rhymes, and chants are wonderful tools for teaching patterns of English language.

- ❖ Children are interested and motivated by music.

- ❖ Musical games provide a context for language.

- ❖ Songs and chants can be used to teach the sounds and rhythms of English.

- ❖ Songs contain many high-frequency words and offer a high degree of repetition.

- ❖ Songs can help children with socialization skills.

- ❖ Music can develop aesthetic tastes and help children express feelings.

- ❖ Auditory learners benefit from being able to listen to themselves sing words.

Activity and Game Suggestions

Musical Vocabulary Chairs

Use a recording that has some of the key vocabulary that you are currently working on in class. For example, if you are learning animal names, use a recording of "Old MacDonald" or "The Farmer in the Dell." Before you begin to play the game, show children photo card illustrations of the key words. Point to the pictures and review the vocabulary. Also, write the vocabulary words on an overhead projector transparency and read the words together to review them.

Next, place the photo cards on the floor in a circle. Have a student stand by each photo card with one extra student. For example, if there are 10 cards, 11 students should be around the circle. Play the music and have children walk around the circle. When the music stops, each child tries to quickly pick up a card. The child left without a card is out. Each child holding a card must then say aloud the key word represented by the picture on the card. Remove one card, have children place the remaining cards on the floor, and play the game again. Repeat until there is only one child left.

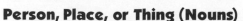

Person, Place, or Thing (Nouns)

Use a recording that has a variety of nouns in the lyrics and find pictures of the featured nouns. Write the lyrics on a transparency for an overhead projector. Review the lyrics together and circle the nouns. Point to the words as children sing the song. Then, use the pictures of the nouns to sort into the noun categories of person, place, or thing.

B-i-n-g-o (or Any Five-Letter Word)

The song "Bingo" is great for teaching any five-letter word. For example, instead of spelling *B-i-n-g-o*, you could sing, "There was a boy who loved candy, and candy is its name. *C-a-n-d-y, c-a-n-d-y, c-a-n-d-y*, and candy is its name."

Learning Names

The chant "Who Stole the Cookies from the Cookie Jar?" is a wonderful tool for children to learn each other's names. Children can recite the following phrases and then take turns choosing a new name.

Everyone: Shalee stole the cookies from the cookie jar.
Shalee: Who, me?
Everyone: Yes, you!
Shalee: Not me!
Everyone: Then, who?
Shalee: Mica stole the cookies from the cookie jar.
Mica: Who, me? *(and the chant continues)*

Add the Missing Words

Teach children a song and then sing it either without the nouns or without the verbs. For example:

(missing nouns)

_____ and _____ went up the _____
To fetch a _____ of _____.
_____ fell down and broke his _____,
And _____ came tumbling after.

(missing verbs)

Jack and Jill _____ up the hill
To _____ a pail of water.
Jack _____ down and _____ his crown,
And Jill _____ _____ after.

Unscramble the Lyrics

Teach children a song. Then, write the song's lyrics on sentence strips for children who are learning to read. Create picture or rebus sentences for emergent readers. Pass out the sentence strips and have children put them in the correct sequence as they sing the song. Here is an example:

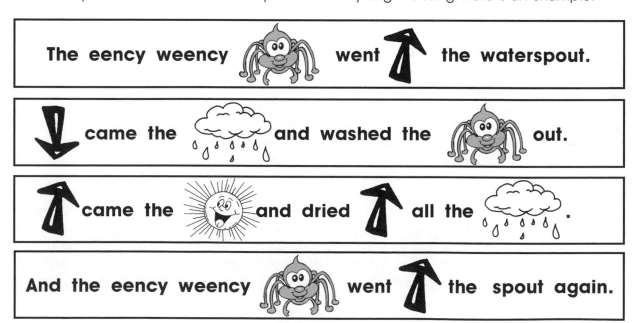

Recommended ELL Song List

- A Tisket, A Tasket *(a green and yellow basket)*
- Alice, the Camel *(had five humps)*
- All Night, All Day *(angels watchin' over me, my Lord)*
- All The Pretty Little Horses *(Hush-a-bye, don't you cry, go to sleep little baby, when you wake)*
- Alphabet Song *(a,b,c,d,e,f,g...)*
- America *(My country 'tis of Thee, sweet land of liberty)*
- America, the Beautiful *(Oh, beautiful for spacious skies)*
- Ants Go Marching, The *(one by one hurrah, hurrah)*
- Bear Went Over the Mountain, The *(to see what he could see)*
- Billy Boy *(Oh where have you been Billy Boy, Billy Boy)*
- Bingo *(There was a farmer, had a dog, and Bingo was his name-o)*
- Blue Tail Fly, The *(Jimmy crack corn and I don't care, my master's gone away)*
- Caissons Go Rolling Along, The *(Over hill, over dale, we will hit the dusty trail, as those)*
- Camptown Races, The *(Camptown ladies sing this song, doo-dah, doo-dah)*
- Crawdad Song *(You get a line, and I'll get a pole honey)*
- Did You Ever See A Lassie? *(a lassie, a lassie, did you ever see a lassie go this way and that)*
- Dixie *(I wish I was in the land of cotton)*
- Down in the Valley *(valley so low, hang your head over)*
- Eency, Weency Spider *(went up the water spout)*
- Farmer in the Dell, The *(the farmer in the dell, hi-ho the dairy-o, the farmer in the dell)*
- Five Little Ducks *(went out to play over the hill and far away)*
- Five Little Monkeys *(jumping on the bed)*
- Frog Went Courtin,' A *(he did ride, with sword and pistol by his side aha, ho-ho)*
- Go Tell Aunt Rhody *(the old gray goose is dead)*
- Go Tell it on the Mountain *(over the hill and everywhere)*
- God Bless America *(land that I love, stand beside her and guide her)*
- Going to the Zoo *(Daddy's taking us to the zoo tomorrow)*
- Head, Shoulders, Knees, and Toes *(knees and toes)*
- Here We Go Round the Mulberry Bush *(so early in the morning)*
- Hickory Dickory Dock *(the mouse ran up the clock)*
- Hokey Pokey, The *(You put your right foot in, you put your right foot out)*
- Home on the Range *(where the deer and the antelope play)*
- Hush Little Baby *(don't say a word, mama's going to buy you a mockingbird)*
- Rock-a-bye Baby *(in the treetops, when the wind blows the cradle will rock)*
- I've Been Swallowed by a Boa Constrictor *(Oh no he's got my toe)*
- I've Been Workin' On the Railroad *(all the live long day)*
- If You're Happy and You Know It *(clap your hands)*
- Looby Loo *(Here we go looby loo, here we go looby light)*
- Mary Had a Little Lamb *(it's fleece was white as snow)*
- Miss Polly Had a Dolly *(who was sick, sick, sick)*
- Muffin Man, The *(Oh, do you know the muffin man)*
- Oats, Peas, Beans, and Barley Grow *(Do you or I or anyone know how oats, peas, beans, and barley grow)*
- Oh! Dear! What Can the Matter Be? *(Johnny's so long at the fair)*
- Oh, Susanna! *(Oh, don't you cry for me)*
- Oh, Where Has My Little Dog Gone? *(Oh where, Oh where can he be)*
- Old Folks at Home *(Way down upon the Swannee River, far, far away)*
- Old MacDonald *(had a farm, e-i-e-i-o)*
- Over the River and Through the Woods *(to grandmother's house we go)*

- ❖ Polly Wolly Doodle *(Oh, I went down south for to see my Sal, singin' polly wolly doodle all the day)*
- ❖ Polly Put the Kettle on *(Polly put the kettle on and we'll all have tea)*
- ❖ Pop, Goes the Weasel! *(All around the cobbler's bench the monkey chased the weasel)*
- ❖ Ring Around the Rosies *(pocket full of posies)*
- ❖ Row, Row, Row Your Boat *(gently down the stream)*
- ❖ She'll Be Comin' Round the Mountain *(when she comes)*
- ❖ Shoo Fly *(don't bother me, shoo-fly don't bother me)*
- ❖ Shortnin-Bread *(Mammy's little baby loves shortnin' shortnin')*
- ❖ Skip to My Lou *(skip to my lou my darling)*
- ❖ Star-Spangled Banner, The *(Oh, say can you see, by the dawn's early light)*
- ❖ Take Me Out to the Ball Game *(buy me some peanuts and crackerjacks)*
- ❖ Ten in Bed *(and the little one said, roll over)*
- ❖ The More We Get Together *(the happier we'll be)*
- ❖ There's A Hole in the Bucket *(dear Liza, dear Liza)*
- ❖ This Land is Your Land *(this land is my land)*
- ❖ This Old Man *(he played one, he played knick-knack on my drum)*
- ❖ Three Blind Mice *(see how they run)*
- ❖ Twinkle, Twinkle Little Star *(how I wonder what you are)*
- ❖ Wheels on the Bus, The *(go round and round)*
- ❖ Where is Thumbkin? *(Where is thumbkin? Here I am)*
- ❖ Yankee Doodle *(went to town riding on a pony, stuck a feather in his cap)*
- ❖ You are my Sunshine *(my only sunshine, you make me happy when skies are gray)*
- ❖ You're A Grand Old Flag *(you're a high flying flag)*

Music/CDs

- ❖ *American Folk, Game & Activity Songs.* Pete Seeger. (Smithsonian Folkways, 2000)
- ❖ *American Folk Songs for Children.* Mike Seeger and Peggy Seeger. (Rounder Select, 1997)
- ❖ *Children's Favorite Songs.* Walt Disney Records. (Disney, 1991)
- ❖ *A Child's Celebration of Songs.* Music for Little People. (Music Little People, 1992)
- ❖ *Little White Duck.* Burl Ives. (Sony Wonder, 1991)
- ❖ *Muppet Hits.* The Muppets. (Zoom Express, 1993)
- ❖ *Old Mr. Mackle Hackle.* Gunnar Madsen. (G-Spot, 1999)
- ❖ *Peter, Paul and Mommy.* Peter, Paul, and Mary. (Warner Bros, 1990)
- ❖ *Raffi Singable Songs Collection.* Raffi. (Rounder, 1996)
- ❖ *Really Silly Songs About Animals.* Bethie. (Discovery House Music, 1993)
- ❖ *Songs to Grow On For Mother and Child.* Woody Guthrie. (Smithsonian Folkways, 1992)
- ❖ *You Sing a Song and I'll Sing a Song.* Ella Jenkins. (Smithsonian Folkways, 1992)

Chapter 4: GAMES
A Natural Way for Children to Learn Language

Think about how all children learn to understand and speak their own native languages—as infants they begin to learn language through listening, responding, and using gestures, sounds, and facial expressions to communicate nonverbally with their parents. Young children listen to stories, music, television, and radio as well as the voices of adults and other children; they live in environments that are filled with language. In other words, native language is learned naturally—through daily experiences with family and friends.

Children who are learning English as a second language or learning English as a foreign language are placed in environments that are not necessarily "natural." They are learning something new and, initially, something that they do not understand. Living in a new country where you do not understand the language can be frightening and frustrating.

Increasingly, vocabulary acquisition is being viewed as crucial to language acquisition. However, new vocabulary has often been taught through the memorization of lists of words, which can become boring for young children, and, let's be honest, is not a lot of fun.

Early childhood educators have known for many years that play is a valuable learning tool. Play can be humorous and entertaining and, at the same time, play can be purposeful in its desired educational outcomes. The playing of games has been found to be a wonderful means of not only teaching and practicing vocabulary, but also of motivating students and increasing fluency.

Research of second language acquisition has shown many areas where learning games have proven to be beneficial and have many advantages for classrooms with ELLs. Here are some of those findings:

* Games can provide a **welcome classroom break** from daily classroom routines.
* Games can be **motivating and entertaining**, which makes the acquisition of learning more likely and more natural.
* Playing games can help **decrease frustration and anxiety levels**, which increases a student's acquisition of comprehensible input.
* When children play games, it is more likely that they will **use language more spontaneously** and not "think" so hard before speaking.
* Games can provide shy or quiet students an **opportunity to express themselves**.
* Games can provide a relaxed atmosphere that is more **conducive to practicing language** in a real-world environment.
* Games can be excellent tools for **introducing new concepts and new ideas**.
* Games can provide young students with **new experiences** that they would not necessarily have during a typical language lesson.
* Playing games allows children to **use language in a meaningful context**.
* Students can **practice listening, speaking, reading, and writing** depending on the games presented by the teacher.

An important tip: Demonstrate how a new game is played by modeling it with one or two students in front of the entire class. This will especially help younger students know what to do to when playing the game. If games require special materials, have children help you create these materials. Their involvement in preparing the game will also help them develop a greater understanding of the language they are learning.

Games for Building Receptive Language

Duck, Duck, Goose

Children love the traditional game of Duck, Duck, Goose. To review the basics of the game, have the children sit in a circle. One child walks around the circle and touches each of the sitting children on the head while saying, "Duck . . . duck . . . duck . . ." and then "goose." The sitting child who was tapped on the word *goose* jumps up and chases the other child around the circle. The tapped child tries to tag the first child before that child can sit down in the empty spot in the circle.

This becomes a fun language game when new vocabulary words are used, such as *cloud, cloud, snow* or *table, table, chair*. It is also fun to use words that have similar consonant or vowel sounds, such as *cat, cat, cow* or *car, car, far*.

Following Directions Train

Have students form a line; each student should hold the waist of the student in front of her. Explain that the students are a train and must travel on the correct train tracks. Use direction words such as *travel faster, travel slower, turn left, turn right, slow down, stop, go*, etc. This is a great game to use to get rid of extra energy or for that three to five minutes before lunch or recess or before it is time to go home.

Charades

Divide the class into two teams. Flip a coin to see which team performs first. The first team sends one of its members to the front of the class. Whisper a word into that student's ear. Then, set a time limit and signal the student to begin pantomiming the word. As soon as one of the team members guesses the word correctly, stop the timer, and the second team takes a turn. The faster team to guess its word wins the round. The team who wins the most rounds is the overall winner of the game.

I Spy

This game can be played outside or in the classroom. Simply say "I spy . . ." and name an object, which the students then search for. The named object (or an attribute of the object) can be a color, number, shape, school tool, piece of clothing, person, toy, or an alphabet/beginning letter sound. The language possibilities are endless.

good Listening and understanding Award

Presented to: _____

Vocabulary Tic-Tac-Toe

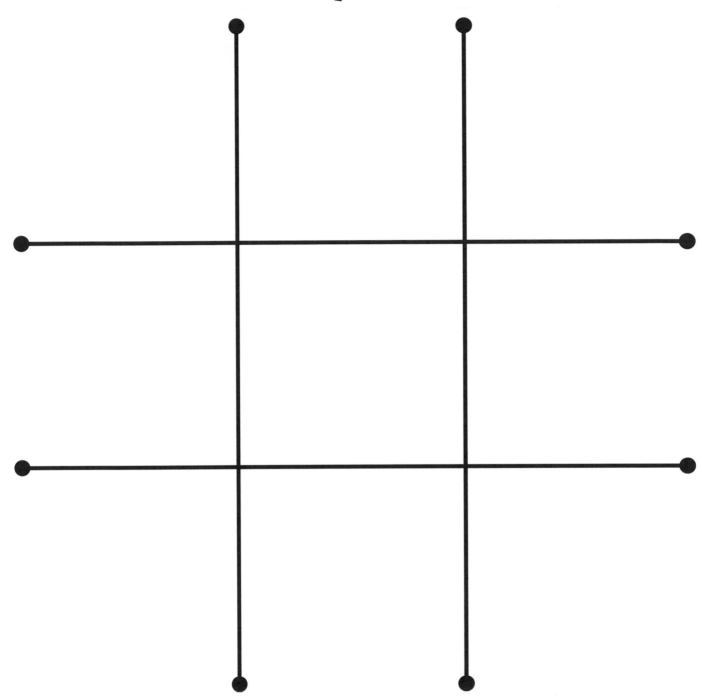

✂ -

Directions: Make one copy of the tic-tac-toe board to use as the master. Fill each box on the master with a picture or word of the vocabulary you are currently working on. Then, copy a page for each student. Following are three ways to play:

1. Play as a group. For example, if you are working on the names of food, fill each square with a food picture or word. As you say the words, children cross out the words they hear. The first child to cross out three in a row wins! *2. Play alone.* Fill the squares with words—however, spell some of the words incorrectly. Children must find and circle the correctly spelled words. *3. Play in pairs.* Place a word or picture in each box. Children will play using the traditional rules of tic-tac-toe, except they must read the word or identify the picture before they can draw an *X* or *O*. Three in a row wins!

BINGO

B	I	N	G	O

Directions: BINGO can be played with any vocabulary.

Student-made BINGO boards: Student-made BINGO boards are a great deal of fun. Reproduce a blank BINGO board for each student. Provide students with a list of 25 or more words. Students may write each word or draw each picture in any square they wish. When the boards are ready, the entire class can play BINGO.

Teacher-made BINGO boards: You can prepare the BINGO boards by making copies of this page and then drawing a picture or writing a word in each square.

Switch Seats

This is an active game that is loads of fun and one that requires good listening skills. Have children sit on chairs in a circle. Stand outside of the circle (so that you can see everyone) and give directions such as:

- ❖ "Children with blue eyes switch seats."
- ❖ "Children with red shirts switch seats."
- ❖ "Children who have baby sisters switch seats."
- ❖ "Children wearing running shoes switch seats."
- ❖ "Children who have pet fish switch seats."

Driving in the Dark–Identifying Left and Right

Create a simple obstacle course in the classroom. First, children should walk through the obstacle course with their eyes open. As students walk through the course, review the vocabulary that you want them to practice, such as *turn left* and *turn right*.

Next, children may go through the obstacle course one at a time with their eyes closed. Children should walk slowly and listen carefully as you direct them to turn either left or right.

Simon Says

Children love to play Simon Says. Here is a review of the **traditional version**. Have children stand in front of you. Children should only follow your direction if you first say "Simon says." If you have not said the words "Simon says," and a child still follows a direction, then that child must sit out. The last child standing is the winner.

Once the children have had the experience of playing the traditional version of Simon Says, you can teach a more **complicated version**. In this version, give two directions at a time. Once the students have mastered following two directions, then give three directions at a time, such as," Touch your knees, touch your shoulders, and then jump."

Whisper, then Draw (Page 23)

This game is very similar to the commercial game Pictionary®. Divide students into teams. Generate a list of words that can be easily illustrated. Or, if you have older or more capable students, they may wish to come up with the list of words. (A reproducible list of Whisper, then Draw words is found on page 24.) Cut the words apart and place them in a box or bag.

Next, choose one team member to do the illustrating and you or another student will be the timekeeper. The student who will draw randomly selects a word from the box or you may whisper a word to the student. The timer is set as soon as the student begins to draw. As the student starts to illustrate the word on large chart paper or on the chalk board, the other students on the team guess what the picture might be. The timer is stopped as soon as the correct answer is given, and the timekeeper writes the time on the board.

(Games for Building Receptive Language)

Whisper, then Draw Word Cards *(Directions are found on page 23.)*

arm	boy	chips	house
ear	girl	eggs	keys
eye	barn	grapes	stove
feet	cat	hamburger	table
hair	chicken	hot dog	vacuum
knee	cow	ice cream	window
nose	dog	milk	blocks
teeth	duck	popcorn	clock
belt	goat	pretzel	crayons
boots	horse	taco	computer
jacket	mouse	bathtub	desk
jeans	pig	book	game
shoes	sheep	broom	homework
pajamas	apple	chair	lunch
t-shirt	bread	comb	paint
baby	cake	cup	paper
mother	carrots	door	pencil
father	cereal	flowers	ruler

KE804071 © Key Education   24   Vocabulary Building Games & Activities

Then, the next team chooses a person to draw and takes a turn. The game can be played for as long as the students maintain interest.

Older or more language proficient students may draw phrases instead of single words. Phrases that utilize a verb and a noun or adverb work well, such as *run fast, jump high, eat breakfast, watch TV, play baseball, ride a bike*, etc.

Whisper, then Draw Word Cards

(Directions are found on page 23.)

arm	boy	chips	house
ear	girl	eggs	keys
eye	barn	grapes	stove
feet	cat	hamburger	table
hair	chicken	hot dog	vacuum
knee	cow	ice cream	window
nose	dog	milk	blocks
teeth	duck	popcorn	clock
belt	goat	pretzel	crayons
boots	horse	taco	computer
jacket	mouse	bathtub	desk
jeans	pig	book	game
shoes	sheep	broom	homework
pajamas	apple	chair	lunch
T-shirt	bread	comb	paint
baby	cake	cup	paper
mother	carrots	door	pencil
father	cereal	flowers	ruler

Games for Building Oral Language

Common Phrases and Gestures

Teaching common phrases that are used every day will encourage your young learners to feel that they are using their new language. Combining gestures with these new phrases will help children understand what the phrases mean and will also help them remember the new words.

Common phrases and corresponding gestures:

Come here ....straighten and then curl index finger
Drink of water ....hold up hand and pretend to drink
Good-bye ....wave
Hello ....wave
I don't know ....lift shoulders and hands
It's cold ....hold arms and shiver
It's hot............................fan face with hand
Listen..............................cup hand behind ear
Look................................point to eyes
Lunch ....pretend to eat
Me ....point to self
No ....turn head side to side
Quiet ....hold finger to mouth and whisper "shhh"
Sit down ....lower hands with palms down
Stand up ....raise hands up with palms up
Stop ....hand up with palm facing out
Toilet ....use the American Sign Language (ASL)
sign for toilet—as shown and then twist
the hand back and forth.

(look)

(toilet)

(lunch)

(listen)

(come here)

Pass It Fast!

Sit with the children in a circle. Show them an object, say the name of the object, and then pass it to the child on your right. That student holds the object, says its name, and then passes it to the next student. To make the game more fun, suddenly change directions, increase the speed, or try passing several objects at once.

Balloon Introductions

Have children stand in a circle and toss a balloon back and forth. When one child taps the balloon, the child says, "What's your name?" The child who catches the balloon says, "My name is . . ." and then taps the balloon to another child while saying "What's your name?" and so on.

Blindfolded Guesses

Place familiar objects in a box. Blindfold children one at a time (or have the children wear very dark sunglasses and close their eyes). The blindfolded child puts a hand in the box and tries to guess the name of the object simply by touching it.

Fun Ideas to Answer Vocabulary Questions

Fly paper airplanes. Have each student make a paper airplane. Designate various areas of the room as targets worth different point values. For example, the chalkboard might be 10 points, your desk 5 points, and so on. Ask one student a vocabulary question. If the question is answered correctly, the student can aim and fly his plane at a target. Have the students keep track of their points.

Shoot the basketball. Ask a vocabulary question. Each time a child's response is correct, the child earns an attempt to shoot the basketball into the hoop. For younger children, tossing crumpled paper or small foam balls into a wastebasket also works well.

Playing Telephone

The traditional game "telephone" is great fun for encouraging oral language. Have children sit in a circle. Whisper a short sentence or phrase to the student next to you. That student then whispers what he heard to the next student and so on. The last student to hear the sentence is asked to repeat out loud what she heard. There are many giggles during this game because, more often than not, the sentence has been radically altered by the end of the line.

Play as a team. Divide the class into two teams. Each team should sit in a circle on opposite sides of the classroom. Whisper the same sentence to the first person on each team. The last team member to listen on each team says the sentence out loud. The team who has relayed the sentence with the fewest changes wins the round.

Play with students who are beginning readers. Write the original sentence on the board. Then, write the sentence the last child heard. Have children compare the written sentences to find what words changed and what stayed the same.

Topic Tag

Post a list of vocabulary words. Choose one student to be "it." "It" chases the other students in hopes of tagging another child who would then become next "it." To avoid being tagged, a child may sit down and say a word from the designated vocabulary list. For example, if the topic is "farm animals," the student being chased would quickly sit down and say the name of a farm animal. If the class was playing "clothing tag," the child would sit down and say the name of a piece of clothing.

What Did You See?

Fill a tray with various objects. Spend a few minutes reviewing the names of the objects on the tray. Take the tray away or cover it with a cloth and then ask children the names of the objects they remember seeing on the tray. There are a variety of ways the game can be played:

Play individually. Ask one child at a time to name everything she can remember seeing on the tray.

Play as a team. Prepare two trays of objects. Divide the children into teams. Show one team a tray and then remove it. What items can that team remember seeing? Show the other team the other tray and remove it. The team who can remember the most objects wins the round.

Write what is remembered. Children who are learning to read and write can write down the names of all the objects they remember seeing.

Music Walk and Talk

Have the students place their chairs in a circle and stand behind them. On each chair, place an object from a current vocabulary unit, such as plastic animals, pictures of classmates, school tools, clothing, etc. Play some music and direct children to walk around the circle while the music is playing. When the music stops, the students must stop and pick up the objects that are on the chairs in front of them. Go around the circle and have children name their objects.

Use more advanced language. For children who are developing more advanced language skills, have those children describe the object, explain what the object is used for, or use the word in a sentence, for example, "I can **comb** my hair," or "I eat with a **spoon**."

List Add On

This is another traditional game that many families play while riding in the car. One person spots something and says its name such as **tree**. The next person must say **tree** and then add another word such as **car**. The next person must then say **tree**, **car**, another word, and so on. The game continues until someone can no longer remember all of the words. You can adapt the game to your classroom by using the vocabulary that you are currently working on.

Learn names. This game can be played to help children learn the names of their classmates during the first week of school or when a new child enters the classroom.

Use more advanced language. For children with more advanced language skills, have them add on words by using all of the words in a sentence. For example:

(Child 1) "I went to the toy store and bought a **red truck**."

(Child 2) "I went to the toy store and bought a **red truck** and a **green pail**."

(Child 3) "I went to the toy store and bought a **red truck** and a **green pail** and a **brown bear**."

Group Guessing

Divide the class into three or four teams. Have each team choose an object from a list of current vocabulary words. One team must guess the object of another team by asking questions such as:

Is it big?   Is it soft?   Is it an animal?   Is it wood?   Can you eat it?

Set a limit on the number of questions that each team may ask. Give a point to the team who guesses the object correctly. If the team is not able to guess, the other team wins the point.

Learn More About Me

This is an active game that helps children learn more about each other and their individual families and cultures. Have the children sit on chairs or on the floor in a circle. Ask one child to volunteer to be first. Ask that child to tell something about himself, about his native country, or something about his family, for example, "I have two brothers." If any other child in the group has two brothers, that child should raise her hand and swap chairs with the child who just shared. Then, that child should share something else about herself, such as, "I am from Mexico." If another child is from Mexico, these two children should swap places.

If several children have the same attribute as the child sharing, they should all swap chairs and each take a turn sharing their information. This game helps children realize that they have things in common with each other, whether it is where they were originally from or simply games that they like to play. Learning that we have more similarities than differences is a fun realization for young children. Be sure to share some of your own information, too.

Fun at the Race Track (Page 28)

Draw a large race track on poster board or use masking tape on the floor to create a track. (See illustration.) Copy the race cars found on page 28, making one car for each child. Let children color, cut out, and decorate their race cars. Laminate the cars for durability.

Use the vocabulary that the students are currently working on to prepare and ask questions. Each time a student correctly answers a question, he can move his car one space on the track.

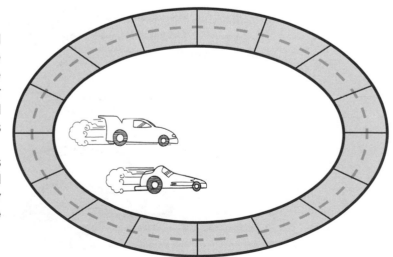

Fun at the Race Track Car Patterns

(Directions are found on page 27.)

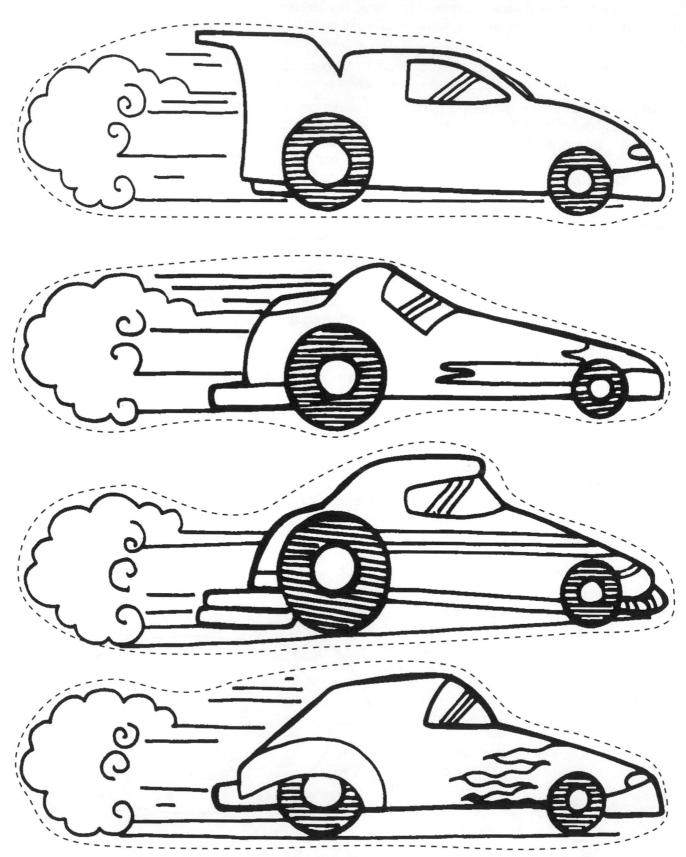

How Well Do We Know Each Other?

Prepare cards, each one describing a different characteristic of children in the class. For example, a card might say *I have two brothers, I have brown eyes, I am eight years old,* or *I have long hair.* You will also need a photograph of each child. Pass out the photographs, making sure that no children get their own photographs.

Choose a description card and read it, or if your students can read, invite a student to choose and read a card. Children should raise their photos up high if they think the description could belong to the child in the photo they are holding. Invite each child to explain how the description fits. For example, "Maria has brown eyes." The description cards will often describe more than one child in the class.

Add a microphone. To add extra fun, use a microphone or make a pretend one. After holding up their photos, children could come to the front of the class and say their descriptive sentences into the microphone. (This can also be scary for some children, so be sure to keep this activity optional.)

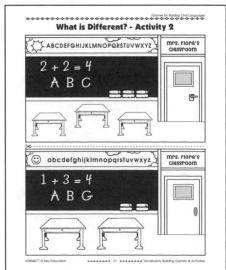

	Animals	Colors	Clothes	People
10	Team 1	___	Team 2	___
20	___	___	Team 2	___
30	___	Team 1	___	Team 1
40	Team 2	___	___	___
50	___	___	___	___

Let's Play "Jeopardy!"

Most teachers are familiar with the game show Jeopardy!® Draw a grid on the chalkboard (see illustration). Choose categories according to the vocabulary students are currently learning. Children can play individually or in teams. The student or team picks a category and the number of points he wants to attempt to win, and you then ask the corresponding question. If the student or team answers correctly, the student's or team's name is written in that space on the grid. If the answer is incorrect, the other player or team gets a chance to answer the question. The game is over when the grid is completely filled. Add up the points to see who is the winner.

What Is Different? (Pages 30 and 31)

This game is a good way to work on vocabulary that describes people and actions as well as using the grammatical structures of *she has* or *he has, they are, there is* or *there are,* and *she is* or *he is* plus an adjective.

Two separate reproducible "What Is Different?" activities are found on pages 30 and 31. Divide children into pairs. For each pair of children, copy one of the pages, cut it in two, and hand the top half to one child and the bottom half to the other child.

At first glance, both half-page pictures look identical. However, there are seven differences between the pictures. Have each pair of children look at their pages and talk about the pictures. For example, one child may say, "There are three desks." The child holding the other picture looks for the desks, sees this is not an identical feature in the picture, and says, "No, there are two desks." The goal is for the pair of children to work together, using language, to discover the seven differences.

You can also easily make your own "What Is different?" pages. Draw a simple picture, copy it, and add seven differences to the photocopied picture.

What Is Different?–Activity 1

(Directions are found on page 29.)

What Is Different?—Activity 2

(Directions are found on page 29.)

Make Your Own Tape Recordings

Practice oral language individually. Children who are shy or quiet often enjoy practicing oral language by themselves. One way to do this is to prepare a tape recording with vocabulary words that need practicing. Say a word or phrase (once or twice) and then pause, leaving a space on the recording before saying the next word or phrase. If you have provided enough space during the pause between each recorded word or phrase, the child will be able to repeat aloud what was just heard without rewinding or stopping the tape.

Use tape recorded listening center games. Another fun idea is to create listening and talking games with teacher-made tape recordings and photographs or illustrated picture cards. First, record all of the names of the cards or say a phrase describing each card. For example, record, "Find the ball," and then say the word *ball* a second time. To play, place all of the cards faceup on the table in random order. The child should listen to the phrase about the ball and then pick up the picture of the ball, repeating the word aloud. To encourage more advanced language, record a descriptive sentence such as, "The children are playing with a ball." Again, the child should find the correct picture and then repeat the entire sentence.

One Word Stories

Play this game with children who have developed a higher level of language skills to encourage critical thinking and using language in grammatical structures.

This simple activity needs no preparation. Sit with students in a large circle. Begin by saying one word. Then, go around the circle, each child adding one more word to create a meaningful sentence. Several sentences will lead to a short story. For example:

Teacher: "I"	Child 3: "animals."	Child 6: "was"	Child 9: "can"
Child 1: "saw"	Child 4: "One"	Child 7: "big."	Child 10:"ride"
Child 2: "many"	Child 5: "animal"	Child 8: "People"	Child 11:"it."

Variations of "Taboo"

The board game Taboo® has become a favorite of language teachers. There are several versions of this game that can be used effectively with students from those with very limited English to students who have a higher degree of language competency. The goal for all of the versions of Taboo is to guess a word by listening to descriptive words. Players cannot use the word to be guessed in any form or use any gestures—those are "taboo!" Here are some fun versions of this game:

Guessing Chair Taboo: One child sits in a chair with her back to the chalkboard. Write a word or tape a picture to the board. The other children take turns saying one word clues while the child in the chair tries to guess the answer.

Guessing Chair Taboo with High Level Language: The game is played as written above with one change. As you write the word to be guessed on the board, add three additional descriptive words (taboo words) that students cannot use as clues. For example, if the word to be guessed is *airplane*, and the three taboo words are *wings*, *fly*, and *pilot*, students must provide clues so that the child in the chair will guess *airplane* without hearing the taboo words as clues. This can be very challenging.

Taboo Teams Provided with Prior Knowledge A: Divide students into teams. Describe five words to each team, giving them solid knowledge of each of these words. Then, mix up the teams and play the game. One student will have a word card and must describe the word so that the other students are able to guess the word.

Taboo Teams Provided with Prior Knowledge B: To prepare students for the vocabulary used in the game, give every child a word or picture card. Each child should privately come to you to learn the proper pronunciation and description of the word. Then, give the children 10 to 15 minutes to swap cards with another student. Both students share the information about their cards. At the end of this collaboration time, the children are better prepared to play the game.

Games for Encouraging Conversations

World Map or Globe

Use a large world map or globe to encourage conversation. Where do people speak Spanish? Where do people live where it is warm? Where is it cold? Who likes cold weather? Who likes warm weather? Where is Australia? Let children take turns locating where they are from. Show them where you were born.

Puppet Theater Conversations

Young children always enjoy playing with puppets and shy children often feel more comfortable talking to puppets than adults. So, begin collecting puppets and buy or build a puppet theater. Both boys and girls love animal puppets. They can facilitate all sorts of fun language, from practicing common phrases such as, "Hello," and "How are you?" to making animal sounds to eventually asking questions of each other and sharing information.

Puppets can become a routine part of your day. Children enjoy holding them as they sing the morning welcome song; puppets can make announcements throughout the day, such as when it is time for lunch or time to clean up; and puppets can be used to introduce new vocabulary.

Conversations with
"Yes, I can . . . ," "No, I can't . . . ," "Yes, I like . . . ," or "No, I don't like . . ."

Play toss and ask. First, have children sit in a circle and practice tossing a ball back and forth. Next, review the sentences of *"Yes, I can . . . ," "No, I can't . . . ," "Yes, I like . . . ,"* and *"No, I don't like . . ."* Make sure children understand the meaning of each of these phrases.

Next, toss a ball to a child and ask a question such as, "Can you swim?" The student catches the ball and answers either, "Yes, I can swim" or "No, I can't swim." That student then tosses the ball to another child and asks the same question and so on. When all of the children have answered the question, begin a new question such as, "Do you like carrots?"

Play without a ball. Play the game as written above except without tossing the ball. Begin by simply asking the question of the child sitting next to you. Go around the circle with one question, listening to the responses. When the question has made the complete circle, ask a new question to begin another round.

Spin the Bottle

This "spin the bottle" game is not the same game that many of you might have played as young teenagers, although the bottle is spun in the same fashion.

Have students sit in a circle on the floor. Spin a plastic soda bottle in the center of the circle. When the bottle stops spinning, it will be pointing to one child. Ask that child a simple question. (Begin with simple questions and then gradually increase the difficulty of the questions.) After a student has answered a question, she gets to spin the bottle for the next turn.

Relay Team Conversations

Divide the children into two teams and direct them to stand in straight lines. The first child in line begins a conversation with the child next to him, such as, "Hello, how are you?" That child turns to the next child in line and might say, "I am fine. Do you want to play?" That child then responds to the next child and so on, until the conversation reaches the end of the line. The first team to have each member contribute to the team conversation is the winner.

Let's Play Vocabulary Battleship

Directions: Copy the battleship grid below for each student. On the chalkboard, write a list of eight to ten words that students are learning and review the words with the students. Have them copy each word into any space on their battleship grids.

Students should choose partners. The partners sit at desks facing each other with their battleship grids on their desks. Stand a book between the students so that they cannot see each other's grids.

The partners ask each other questions such as, "Is there a word on C4?" If there is a word on that space, the student gets a "hit" and learns what the word is. If there is not a word on C4, the student records a "miss." The first player to discover all of his partner's words is the winner!

Battleship Grid

	A	B	C	D	E	F	G	H	I
1									
2									
3									
4									
5									
6									
7									
8									
9									

Games for Early Readers

Label Everything

It is a great idea to label everything, especially for students who are new to this country and need a quick introduction to the necessary vocabulary for school. Write words for everything in the room on card stock or index cards. Spend some time daily for several days reading the words on the cards.

When you think children are becoming familiar with the words, remove the cards, shuffle them, and hand them out to the students. Have students put the cards by the correct objects. Later, surprise your students and place all of the cards by incorrect objects. Who was the first student to notice that the cards were in the wrong places? Then, have students correct all of the mistakes.

Hanging Up Words to Build Sentences

This is a fun hands-on activity that can even be played with students who have a limited English reading vocabulary. String up a clothesline, have a basket of spring clothespins, and prepare word T-shirts. Copy the T-shirt pattern below on colored card stock, choosing colors for different parts of speech, for example, red for nouns, blue for verbs, and so on. Write a word on each shirt. Let the children hang up the words to form sentences.

T-Shirt Pattern

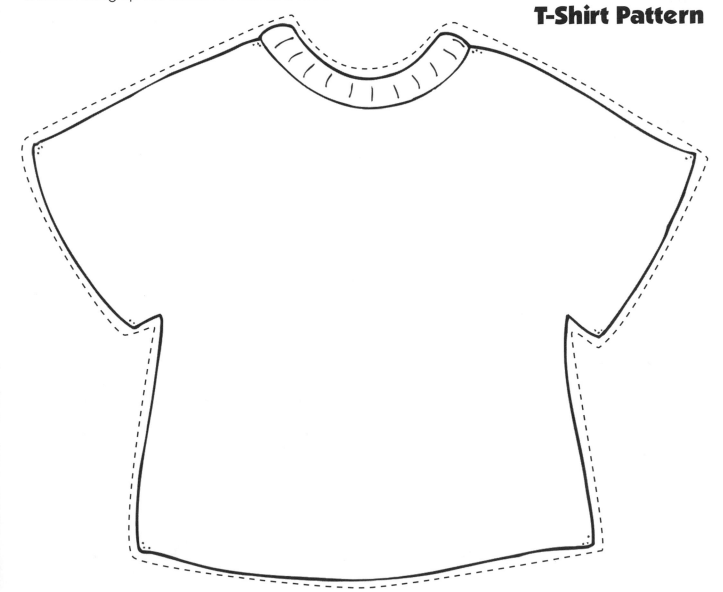

Spelling Snakes

Students need to have a good understanding of beginning and ending consonant sounds. Say a word such as *dog*, emphasizing the final consonant *g*. The next student must come up with a word that begins with the ending sound /g/, such as *goat*. The next student then needs a word that begins with /t/, such as *ten*, and so on.

dog — goat — ten — nut — took — keep

Hang the Spider (Page 37)

Copy page 37. This page will be shared and played with partners. The first child thinks of a word and draws a line for each letter of the word in the word box. The second child tries to figure out what the chosen word is by guessing letters. (Each letter should be crossed off on the alphabet below the spider as it is guessed.) If a letter is guessed correctly, that letter is printed on the correct line in the word box. For each wrong guess, the first child may color one body part of the hanging spider. The second child tries to identify the word before the spider is completely colored.

Teacher Made Word Searches

Place new vocabulary words into a word search or crossword puzzle. There are many good Internet sites that can help you create these puzzles. Children especially enjoy looking for words in a word search. It is also fun to turn the word search puzzles into transparencies to be used on an overhead projector. Children like to write on transparencies and the entire class can participate in locating the words.

Read the News!

Cut out photographs and advertisements from a newspaper. Ask children what they think each picture is about. What would make a good headline? What is the picture advertising? Encourage the use of new vocabulary words during the discussion.

Human Letters

Create a list of new words for the students to learn. Have letter cards available—every letter in every word should be represented. For example, for the words *cat*, *cow*, and *car*, you would need three *c* cards, two *a* cards, one *t* card, one *o* card, one *w* card, and one *r* card. Pass out all of the letter cards, say a vocabulary word, and have students come to the front of the room if they have one of the letters in the word. Students should then arrange themselves in the correct sequence to spell the word. If two children have the same letter and only one is needed, they need to decide which one of them should stay to spell the word.

Jumbled Sentences

Write a sentence on a sentence strip and cut apart the individual words. You can also write each of the sentence's words on index cards. The goal is for children to take the words and arrange them into a meaningful sentence.

First, tell children a short story. For example, read the story "The Three Little Pigs" and write and cut apart the sentence "The little pig built a house of sticks." Hand out the individual words, making sure students can read all of the words and understand each word's meaning.

Help students assemble the jumbled sentence with some clues. For example, the first word is the one with the capital letter. The last word is followed by a punctuation mark.

Name _____

Hang the Spider

(Directions are found on page 36.)

Word Box

a	b	c	d	e	f	g	h	i	j	k	l	m

n	o	p	q	r	s	t	u	v	w	x	y	z

Vocabulary Tree

The Vocabulary Tree on page 39 is actually a vocabulary chart—a type of graphic organizer that helps students expand their passive and active vocabularies. This type of chart helps students see (which helps them remember) new vocabulary.

Copy page 39 for students. You may also create a transparency of the tree that can be used effectively for demonstration on an overhead projector. (See the example illustrated on the right.)

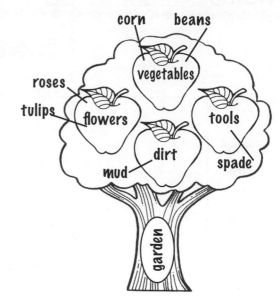

Comic Books

Cut out short comic strips from the daily paper. Select comics with simple vocabulary and humor that the children can understand, such as *Peanuts*. First, cover up the text so that only the pictures are visible. Discuss what is happening in each vignette and have children guess what might be funny about the cartoon.

Then, show children the words. Read the comic strip as a group. The cartoon can be spontaneously acted out and the whole class can laugh together. Discuss if the children's guesses were correct about what they thought might be funny in the comic.

Keep a collection of the comic strips and attach them to pieces of card stock. Combine the pages into a classroom comic book that children can read and chuckle over again and again!

Create a comic book bulletin board. Use the pattern below to create captions and write short dialogue.

Speech Bubble Pattern

Vocabulary Tree

(Directions are found on page 38.)

Chapter 5: REPRODUCIBLE WORD AND PHOTO CARD GAMES

Reproducible word and photo cards are included In each of the 22 thematic units found in Chapter 6 beginning on page 45. The cards can be used as flash cards for practice and review and they can also be used to play the educational games described in this chapter.

How to Prepare the Reproducible Word and Photo Cards

To prepare the word and photo cards for use, first copy the cards on card stock and laminate them for durability. For quick reference, copy each unit's cards on a different color of card stock (preferably pastel colors) and organize them in an index card box for storage and easy retrieval.

Games to Play

Memory Match

General directions: Place the cards facedown on a table or floor. Children will take turns flipping over two cards at a time. The child should say the name of the photo or read the word each time a card is turned over. If the cards match, the child keeps the matching pair of cards. If the cards do not match, they are placed facedown again, and the next child takes a turn.

Here are a variety of ways to play memory match:

- ❖ *Variation 1:* **Match two identical photo cards.** Make two copies of each photo card to play.

- ❖ *Variation 2:* **Match two identical word cards.** Make two copies of each word card to play.

- ❖ *Variation 3:* **Match a word card to a photo card.** Make one copy of each photo card and each word card to play.

Sorting and Classifying Cards

Show children four picture cards. Three of the cards should go together while one card does not belong, for example, *cat, dog, car,* and *fish.* Ask which picture does not belong and, if children have enough language, to explain why. If children are reading, also play this game with word cards.

Card Walking

Place many cards on the floor in a circular path around the room. Play some music as children follow the path of cards. When the music stops, have children pick up the cards in front of them and take turns saying aloud what is on each card. If a child answers correctly, the child keeps the card. If the answer is incorrect, the card is returned to the floor. When all of the cards have been picked up, children may count their cards to see who has collected the most!

What's Missing?

Lay six to ten cards faceup on a table or propped on a blackboard ledge. Have children look at the cards for one minute and then close their eyes. Remove a card. Invite children to open their eyes and ask them, "What's missing?" The child who correctly identifies the missing card is the next child to remove one of the cards.

Variation: To increase the difficulty, after a card is removed, rearrange the remaining cards.

Who Has It?

Pass out two or three cards to each child. Call out the picture or word that is on one of the cards. The child who has the card should stand up and repeat the word. Play until all of the cards have been called out and identified by the children.

Leap to the River

Place some masking tape on the classroom floor to create an imaginary river (see illustration). Label one side of the river with the word **right** and the other side with **wrong**. Explain to children that they will be in a boat on the river. Have children play one at a time. Hold up either a word or photo card (depending on the ability levels of your students) and say what is on the card, varying between saying the word correctly and incorrectly. The child must decide if you are right or wrong and then jump to the correct side of the river.

Up 'n' Back Racing

Line up cards at one end of the classroom. Have children line up in teams at the other end of the room. Call out one of the words. The first child in line for each team dashes to the cards, tries to be first to find and grab the correct card, and then returns to the team. When all of the cards are collected, have the teams count their cards. The team with the most cards wins!

Question and Answer Cards

This game requires some teacher preparation. Make a list of the vocabulary words children are working on and find a photo or word card for each. Next, prepare question cards—one question for each vocabulary word. To play, pass out to each student two or three photo or word cards, which will serve as answer cards. Place all of the question cards in a hat or facedown in a pile.

Draw a question card and read it. Have children look at their cards. The child who is holding the photo or word card that answers the question reads it aloud and gives it to you. The first child to give up all of her cards is the winner.

Here are some examples of question and answer cards:

Question: What do we use to wash our hands?	*Answer:* soap
Question: What shows us the time of day?	*Answer:* clock
Question: Where do we sleep?	*Answer:* bed
Question: What should you wear when it is cold outside?	*Answer:* coat or sweater

Memory Magician

Choose one child to be the Memory Magician. The Memory Magician must pay very close attention to play this game. First, place six to ten cards faceup on a tabletop. Ask the same number of children to look at the cards. Each child should choose a different card and—without touching it—say the name of the card aloud. When the children have each said the name of one of the cards, the Memory Magician picks up all of the cards, walks to each child, and hands the card that the child named to that child. The more cards you use, the more difficult the game becomes.

Watch It Appear!

Hold a photo card behind a book or flannel board. Move the card up slowly so that the children can only see a small part of the card at first. Gradually, more and more of the card should become visible to the children. Invite children to call out what they think is pictured on the card. The first child to guess correctly is the next person to hold and move up a photo card.

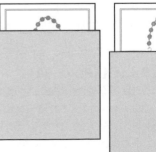 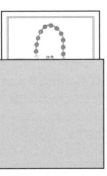 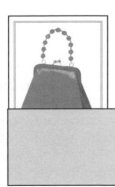

Giant Word/Photo Card Game Board

Learning new vocabulary is tons of fun when children get to play on a giant game board. This idea can be used to practice any vocabulary words children are currently learning.

What you will need: First, choose a large number of word or photo cards. Lay the cards on the floor in a game board design. Often, children want to keep this game set up for days, so it is best to put it in an area of your classroom that will not be disturbed. Include extra spaces of plain colored paper in addition to the word/photo card spaces and spaces for *start* and *finish*. You will need a die and a game marker, for example, a small toy car, eraser, or math counter, for each player.

How to play: Each player rolls the die. The player with the largest number begins the game. That player then rolls the die and moves his marker that number of spaces. If the player lands on a word/photo card space the player must say the word. If the player correctly identifies the vocabulary word, his marker can remain on that space. If the player is wrong, he must move his marker back to the previous space. The first player to reach the finish space is the winner! See the following variations for more advanced students:

❖ ***Variation 1:*** Have players use the vocabulary word in a sentence.

❖ ***Variation 2:*** Have players describe the use of the vocabulary word.

❖ ***Variation 3:*** Have players describe attributes of the vocabulary word.

Drawing Races

Divide students into two teams and have each team form a line. Whisper a vocabulary word into the ear of the first student in each line. On the word "go," those students should race to the chalkboard and draw a picture of the word that was whispered in their ears. The first team to guess what the picture is wins that round and is awarded a point. The game ends when every child has had an opportunity to draw a vocabulary word. The team with the most points wins.

Run and Shout It!

Divide students into two groups. Have the groups stand on either side of the room in two lines facing each other. Assign every student on each team a number beginning with one. Place a large variety of word/photo cards in the center of the room. Call out a number and the name of a word/photo card. The students from each team who are assigned that number run into the center, touch the card, and shout out the vocabulary word. The first child to touch the card brings it back to her team. The game ends when all of the cards have been picked up. The team with the most cards wins!

Look Fast!

Tell children they will need to keep their eyes on you! Pick up a word or photo card and flash it quickly before the students. The students shout out what word or picture they think was on the card. Children think this is a lot of fun, and it forces them to pay close attention.

Hot Potato

This traditional game has been enjoyed by children for many years. Invite children to sit in a circle. Give four or five of the children a word or photo card. Have children pass the cards around the circle while listening to music. When the music stops, each child holding a card must name the vocabulary word on the card.

Design Your Own Game Board (Page 44)

The game board on page 44 can be used to practice any vocabulary words. Make one copy of the game board. Then, draw pictures or write words in each blank. Students may also wish to make their own game boards. Follow the game directions from the Giant Word/Photo Card Game Board activity above.

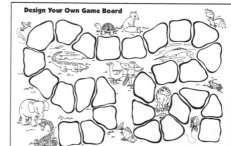
Design Your Own Game Board

Sentence Teams

Divide your students into two teams. Give each team a timer. Lay out an assortment of word/photo cards. Have one student from each team choose a card. If the player uses the word in a sentence in under 10 seconds that team is awarded a point. If the player is unable to use the word in a sentence or takes longer than 10 seconds, that team does not receive any points.

Decrease the time by one second for each following round of play. For example, the second round of players would have to use the word in a sentence in nine seconds, round three would be eight seconds, and so on.

Slam: Truth or Lies

This is a good game for a small group of students. Prepare a deck of pairs of matching word and photo cards. Pass out all of the cards to the players—making sure that no player has more than six cards. The object of this game is to be the first player to get rid of all of his cards.

Player A tosses one of his cards facedown on the table and says to player B on his right, "I have a **chair.**" If player B already has two chair cards, she knows player A is lying and then can say, "No, you don't have a chair." But, if player B does not have any chair cards or has just one chair card, she must guess whether or not player A is telling the truth.

If player B guesses correctly (and is not tricked by player A), player B gives player A one of her cards. If player B guesses wrong, then player A gives player B one of his cards. Play continues with each player attempting to trick the player on his right.

Go Fish

This is a traditional card game that children love to play. Prepare four identical sets of cards and mix them up to create one deck of cards. Children will try to get identical pairs of cards.

Pass out four cards to each player with the remaining cards placed facedown on the table as the "fish pond." Player A asks a question of one of the other players, for example, "Do you have an **apple**?" If the player has an apple card, he must give that card to player A, and player A can then lay down the pair of identical apple cards. If the player does not have an apple card, he says, "Go fish." Player A then draws a card from the fish pond.

If player A gets the card she asked for, she receives another turn. The play passes to the next player if player A does not get the card she asked for. The player with the most pairs of cards is the winner.

Where's My "Go-Together?"

Organize word/photo cards that go together in pairs. There are many possibilities for playing this game, such as:

- ❖ **Variation 1:** A consonant letter card and a photo card whose name begins with that consonant sound

- ❖ **Variation 2:** Opposites cards such as many and few or wet and dry

- ❖ **Variation 3:** Go-together cards such as paper and pencil, fork and spoon, table and chair, or shoes and socks

Pin a card on the back of each child. Have children move around the room looking at the backs of their classmates while trying to discover which children have their matches. Time the children. How long does it take for all of them to find their go-together matches?

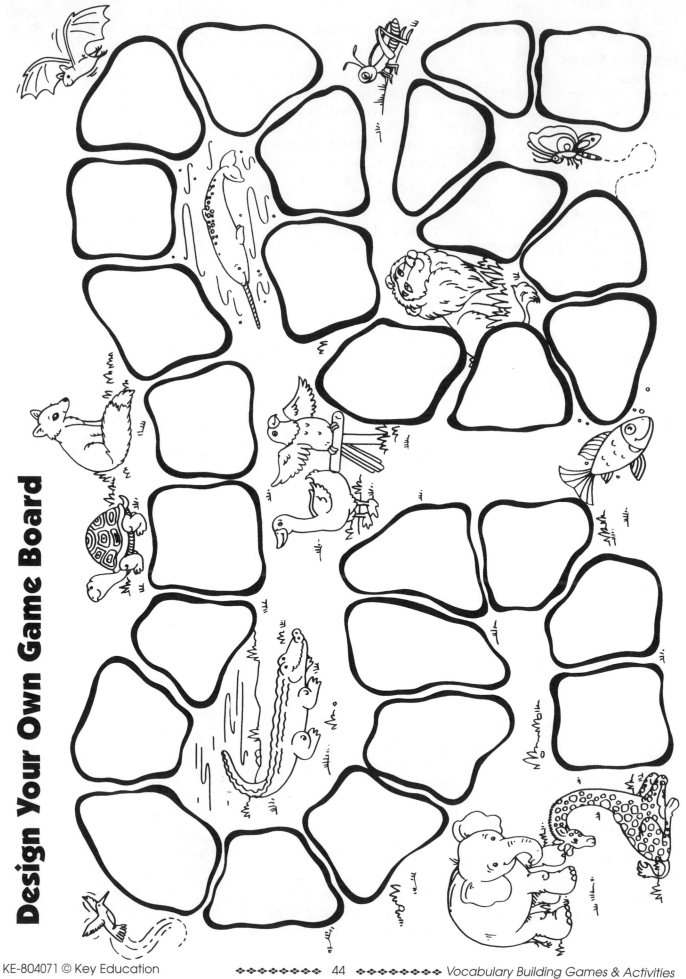

Design Your Own Game Board

Unit 1: All About Me/ Getting to Know Each Other

The Welcome and Beginning Phrases

Start by welcoming each child individually into the classroom. To get everyone off to a great start, begin by teaching a few phrases to help children adjust emotionally and socially. Phrases such as, "hello," "good-bye," "My name is . . . ," and "It is nice to meet you" along with crucial personal information, such as the child's address and phone number, help children to be able to meet and greet people. It will also assist them to remember survival information in case they need to explain where they live or how to call home. (See the vocabulary cards on pages 48 and 49.)

Begin everyday the same. Use the same welcome phrase every morning, such as, "Good morning. How are you?" After a very short time, children will begin to repeat the welcome phrase back to you. At first, you will need to prompt the correct response to the phrase, such as, "Fine, thank you," but very quickly children will be saying the response back to you. This exchange will give them a sense of achievement and self-confidence. It will also make the "English" classroom a special place, and they will look forward to being a member of this wonderful class.

Hello Songs

Most young children love to sing! A welcome song that is interactive will be greeted with much enthusiasm. It is also a great signal to let children know that the school day is beginning. Use a song like "Where is . . . ?" that has an easy-to-remember melody and lots of repetition. This song can also help children learn each other's names. The following songs are good ways to start your day:

Where is . . . ?
(sung to the tune of Frère Jacques)
Teacher: Where is (student's name)?
               Where is (student's name)?
Student: Here I am. Here I am.
Teacher: How are you (student's name)?
Student: I am fine. Thank you.
Everyone: We are glad you are here.
(Then, sing to another child.)

Happy School Day
(sung to the tune "Happy Birthday to You")
Happy school day to you!
We will learn something new!
Hello, sun,
We will have fun,
Happy school day to you!

A Great "Anytime" Song
Oh, the more we get together,
together, together,
Oh, the more we get together,
the happier we'll be.
For your friends are my friends,
And my friends are your friends.
Oh, the more we get together,
the happier we'll be.

The Name Game

Begin with everyone standing in a circle. Children need to be able to see one another. Each child will take a turn saying his name and doing an action at the same time. The action could be waving a hand, taking a bow, etc. Each child's action should be different. It's natural for children to all want to do the same thing, but make it clear that, for this activity, they need to do their own actions. Go around the circle with children saying their names and doing their actions. When you have been around the circle twice, say someone else's name and try to perform that person's action. The person you choose must then say someone else's name and do the person's action. Continue until everyone's name has been said and action performed.

All About Me

Once children are starting to feel at ease in an English classroom, you can move on to your first topic, "All About Me/Getting to Know Each Other." Keeping it personal helps children relate to the topic. They can talk about their names and the names of their native countries. Locate each country on a globe or map. Children should leave the classroom feeling as though they have achieved something.

Large Self-Portraits

Draw a picture of yourself on a large piece of paper. Ask children if they know whose picture it is. Then, point to yourself with a big smile and write your name at the bottom of the picture. Hand out paper and crayons to children and ask them to draw pictures of themselves. Write the children's names on their pictures. When they have finished, show them your picture again and say, "My name is _____." Then, go around the class and encourage each child to hold up her picture and say her name. Ask, "What is your name?" Then, model the response, "My name is _____."

My Own Box or Cubbie

Provide each of the students with a shoe box. Have children draw small pictures of themselves to place on the ends of their boxes. Explain to children that these are their own boxes and that they can keep their own things in them. Make yourself a box and put some things inside it to show the children, such as pencils, a pen, a comb, a picture of your family or pet—things that are obviously your own.

Children will enjoy adding things to their boxes, such as pictures of some of their favorite things—books, toys, their families, and so on. The boxes are also fun to share with parents on parent evenings at school or at parent/teacher conferences.

All About Me Minibook (Page 47)

Before beginning the lesson, obtain the students' current addresses and keep them in a convenient place. Many newcomers have frequent changes of address. For children to understand the significance of their addresses and phone numbers is crucial. Show children a letter or an envelope on which an address has been printed and say, "This is an address" as you point to it. Say, "Each home has an address." Ask a student to volunteer to recite her address from memory. Younger students may need a great deal of practice. Older students need to learn to write their addresses and phone numbers. All of this critical information should be reviewed frequently.

Copy page 47 for each child. Have children fill in the information and color the pictures. Cut out the minibooks along the dashed lines and then fold them along the solid lines.

(Cut along the dotted lines. Fold along the solid lines.)

-3-

Write your phone number.

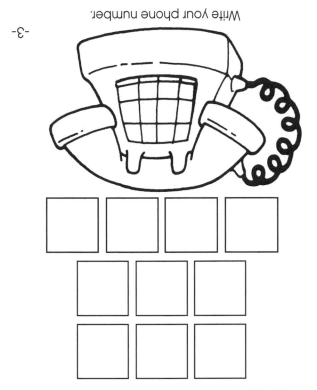

My phone number is

-2-

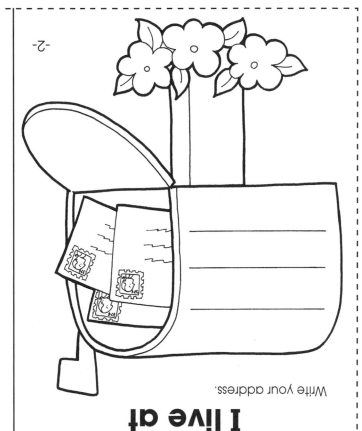

Write your address.

I live at

I am ____ years old.

Draw the correct number of candles on the cake.

-4-

My name is

This is me.

-1-

What is your name?

My name is _____.

Where do you live?

I live at _____.

What is your phone number?

My phone number is _____.

I am a boy.

I am a girl.

Hello.

Good-bye.

How are you?

Fine, thank you.

This is my friend _____.

Nice to meet you.

Unit 2: Alphabet

Reproducible Letter and Photo Cards

The reproducible cards found on pages 54 to 62 can be used in all of the following games and activities. They can also be used to make a variety of memory-matching games, such as:

- ❖ match uppercase to uppercase letters
- ❖ match lowercase to lowercase letters
- ❖ match uppercase to lowercase letters
- ❖ match a letter card to a picture representing a beginning letter sound

Reproducible Letter and Photo Card Games

Alphabet Yell

Randomly pick up an alphabet letter card and show it to the class. The first student to correctly shout out the name of that letter gets a point. Later on, as children become more familiar with the letters of the alphabet, have them shout out words that begin with the letter on the card you are holding.

Alphabet Printing Relay

Divide students into two teams and have them stand in two lines. Draw a line down the middle of the chalkboard. Starting at the beginning of the alphabet, have one student from each team run up to the chalkboard, write **A**, and run back to the end of the line. The next two students in the lines then run up and write **B**. The first team to finish writing the entire alphabet wins.

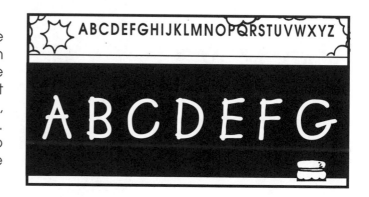

Erase the Letters Relay

This game is similar to Alphabet Printing Relay above. Divide students into two relay teams. Draw a line down the middle of the chalkboard and print the entire alphabet on each side of the line. Starting at the beginning of the alphabet, have one student from each team run up to the chalkboard, erase **A**, and run to the back to the end of the line. The next two students in the lines then run up and erase **B**. The first team to finish erasing the entire alphabet wins.

First letter

This is a good beginning activity. Hand out alphabet letter cards, one to each student. Tell students you will say the alphabet and ask them to hold up their alphabet cards when they hear you say their letters.

Alphabet Sculptures

Divide students into teams and call out the name of an alphabet letter or show the students an alphabet letter card. The first team that can work together to form the shape of the letter with their bodies wins a point. The team with the most points wins!

I Spy Letters or Letter Sounds

The purpose of this game is letter name or letter sound recognition. It can be played as a relay race or individually.

Variation 1: Hold up an alphabet letter card. The students must look all around the classroom to find that same letter written somewhere in the room.

Variation 2: Hold up an alphabet letter card. The students must look all around the classroom to find an object that begins with that letter sound.

My Own Alphabet Dictionary

An alphabet dictionary can help children increase their oral vocabularies as well as help them learn the alphabet and strengthen some beginning reading skills. Introduce a letter a day (or week) and print it on the board. Then, print three small words beginning with the letter for students to copy in their own alphabet dictionaries. This is also a book they can take home and share with their parents.

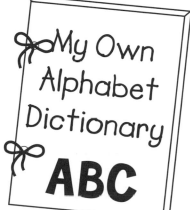

- ❖ Organize the words ahead of time. Plan how you want to introduce them and how you will explain each word's meaning so that your young ELLs will understand and remember the words.
- ❖ Introduce nouns to younger children. Students can draw a picture of each noun next to the written word. Nouns are much easier than adjectives or verbs for young children to depict with a drawing.
- ❖ Bring in objects that represent the chosen letter of the day or week.

Let's Pretend to Make Alphabet Soup

Place plastic letters in a bowl. Use the photo cards on pages 54 to 62 of objects whose names begin with those same letters. Let each student draw a plastic letter from the bowl and then find the photo card that begins with that letter.

Squeeze Puffy Paint Alphabet Letters

You will need: flour, salt, liquid tempera paint, card stock or cardboard, empty squeeze bottles with narrow nozzles, mixing bowls, paper towels

What you do: Mix equal parts of flour, salt, and water together in a bowl. Add tempera paint for color. Mix well and pour into the squeeze bottle. Squeeze the puffy paint onto cardboard or heavy stock paper. The mixture will become hard when it dries.

No-Cook Baker's Clay Alphabet Letters

You will need: 4 cups flour, 1 cup salt, 1 teaspoon powered alum, 2 cups water, food coloring

Special Tip: If you prefer an even distribution of color, add the food coloring to the water before the water is mixed with the other ingredients.

What you do: Mix the flour, salt, and powdered alum together. Slowly mix the water into the flour mixture and then knead it for several minutes. Divide the dough into smaller balls and then add a different food coloring to each section of dough. Store in airtight containers. Use alphabet letter cookie cutters or create your own letter shapes.

Place letter shapes on an ungreased cookie sheet and bake for 30 minutes in an oven set at 250°F (121°C). Turn the shapes over and bake them for another 30 minutes.

Letters in the Air

Print an alphabet letter on the chalkboard. Direct students to stand and look at the board. Raise your finger and trace the letter in the air. This will actually help children learn to visualize the letter.

Alphabet Song

Children love "The ABC Song," and it really does seem to be an effective way to teach the sequence of alphabet letters. Assign each student a letter and have students make their own letter flash cards. Sing "The ABC Song" and invite students to hold up their letters when the letter names are sung.

A, B, C, D, E, F, G,
H, I, J, K, L, M, N, O, P,
Q, R, S,
T, U, V,
W, X,
Y, and Z
Now I know my ABC's.
Next time, won't you sing with me?

Additional Song Ideas:

❖ Give each student a few sequential alphabet letter cards and play "The ABC Song." Have students hold up the cards that correspond to the letters they hear in the song.

Alphabet Desk Tape (Page 53)

Copy for each student the reproducible alphabet desk tape found on page 53. Let the children color each section, cut out along the dashed lines (do not cut the solid lines), and tape the sections together to form one long alphabet desk tape. The pictures (representing the letter sounds) on the desk tape are everyday words that young Ell students will need to learn.

Here is the word key for the alphabet desk tape:

a= apple	e=egg	i=inch	m=money	q=quiet	u=uniform
a=ate	e=eat	i=ice	n=name	r=ruler	v=video
b=book	f=family	j=jump	o=octopus	s=sing	w=walk
c=computer	g=girl	k=key	o=open	t=table	x=eXit
d=desk	h-hand	l=library	p=paper	u=up	y=yard
					z=zipper

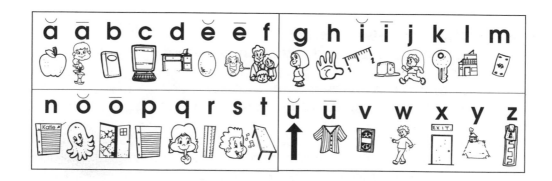

(Directions found on page 52.)

Alphabet Desk Tape

ă ā b c d ĕ ē f

n ŏ ō p q r s t

g h ĭ ī j k l m

ŭ ū v w x y z

Alphabet Puzzles

Copy the letter and photo cards found on pages 54–62. Cut them out in sections of three cards (uppercase letter, lowercase letter, and photo card, as shown). Do not cut the cards apart on the straight vertical lines. Cut them apart using zigzag or curved lines to create either two-piece or three-piece puzzles.

To create self-checking puzzles, draw a line or design on the back of the puzzles section. The children can turn over the puzzles to see if they have a correct match.

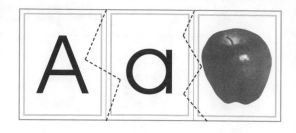

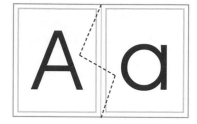
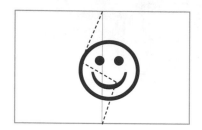
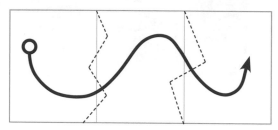

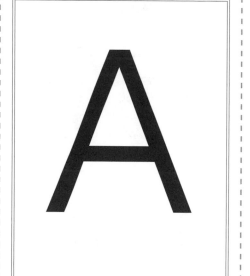

C c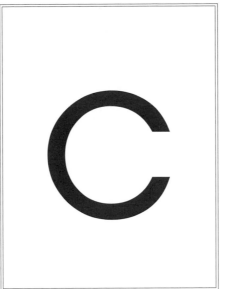

D d

E e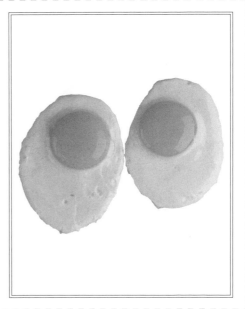

F

f

G

g

H

h

I

i

J

j

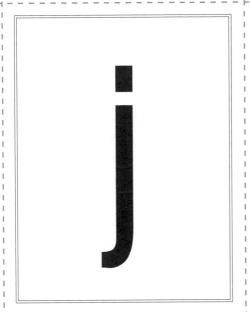

K

k

L

l

M

m

N

n

O o

P p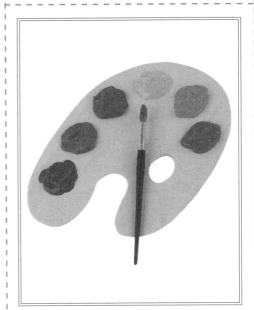

Q q

R

r

S

s

T

t

U

u

V

V

W

W

X

x

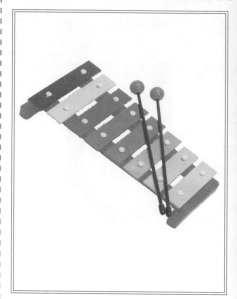

Y

y

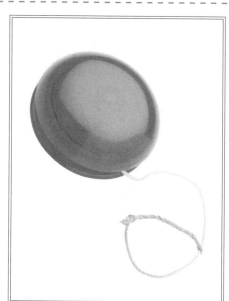

Z

z

Unit 3: Body Parts

Introduction

The words for body parts are important for young children to learn. Children need this vocabulary to describe where they are hurt or if they are not feeling well. See the word and photo cards on pages 66 to 72 for a complete list of the words to be introduced.

Making Funny Faces/Introduction of Facial Features Vocabulary

Provide old magazines or catalogs and have students cut out photographs of human facial features. If your students are very young, you may want to cut out the pictures yourself. Children who have some scissor skills will enjoy looking for the photographs and cutting them out. Be sure to have many magazines and catalogs to search through so that children have lots of facial features from which to choose.

Then, have each child draw a circle and paste on the facial features. Hair can be yarn attached with glue, or it can be drawn and colored in. These faces look very funny, and the children have a lot of fun making them.

Doctor Says/Introduction of Body Parts Vocabulary

Tell children it is important to be able to name all of their body parts. If they are hurt, they can tell someone what parts of their bodies are hurting. Help children to practice naming body parts by playing Doctor Says.

This game is played just like Simon Says, only begin each direction children should follow with, "Doctor says, touch your *(name a body part)*." Children only touch the part if the "Doctor says."

Shadows

Use a freestanding projector screen or hang up a sheet. Place a lamp behind the screen and turn off all other lights. Have the class sit facing the front of the screen. Let children take turns going behind the screen. The children in front of the screen will be able to see the child's shadow. The child behind the screen can choose how she wants to move, for example, dance, wiggle, sway or jump.

Variation 1: Instruct the child to move one body part at a time. For example, a child may shake his head, wave a hand, or tap a foot. The other children can describe what the child is doing using body parts vocabulary.

Variation 2: Ask children who are sitting in front of the screen to close their eyes. Choose one child to stand behind the screen and move. The other children open their eyes and, without looking around at their classmates, try to guess who is behind the screen.

Real-Size Me!

Have children take turns lying on a large piece of butcher paper and having a friend trace around them. The children should then color their pictures to look just like them. Review body part names as the children work. Display the pictures around the classroom or in the hall.

Additional idea: Ask for a volunteer and trace around that child's body. Each time you introduce a new body part word, print the word by that body part on the large drawing.

Great Songs for Teaching Body Parts Vocabulary

Five Little Monkeys Jumping on the Bed
Five little monkeys jumping on the bed,
One fell off and bumped his head.
Mama called the doctor and the doctor said,
"No more monkeys jumping on the bed!"

Four little monkeys jumping on the bed,
One fell off and bumped his head.
Mama called the doctor and the doctor said,
"No more monkeys jumping on the bed!"

(and the song continues)

Head, Shoulders, Knees, and Toes
Head, shoulders, knees, and toes,
Knees and toes.
Head, shoulders, knees, and toes,
Knees and toes.
Eyes and ears and mouth and nose,
Head, shoulders, knees, and toes

Add some new verses:

Five little monkeys leaping chair to chair,
One fell off and pulled her hair . . .

Five little monkeys ran through the barn,
One fell down and broke his arm . . .

Five little monkeys were doing the twist,
One fell down and broke his wrist . . .

Five little monkeys climbing a tree,
One fell off and skinned his knee . . .

Five little monkeys running on a track,
One fell down and hurt his back . . .

Five little monkeys playing on a boulder,
One fell off and bumped his shoulder . . .

Five little monkeys skipping in the sand,
One fell down and scraped his hand . . .

I'm Being Swallowed by a Boa Constrictor
I'm being swallowed by a boa constrictor
I'm being swallowed by a boa constrictor
I'm being swallowed by a boa constrictor
And I don't like it very much!
Oh no, he's got my toe,
Oh gee, he's got my knee,
Oh my, he's got my thigh,
Oh fiddle, he's got my middle,
Oh heck, he's got my neck,
Oh dread, he's got my . . . (gulp!)

Body Buddy Boogie
(sung to the tune of "Red River Valley")
Touch your head,
Touch your ears,
Touch your elbows!
Reach your hands
Way up high to the sky.
Wave your arms,
Stamp your feet,
Puff your cheeks out.
Then, stand with your head
Held up high!

Wiggle your fingers,
Then, clap hands!
Now put your hands
On your hips.
Touch your nose,
Touch your neck,
Bend your wrists back,
And then make a big smile
With your lips!

Body Parts Puzzle

Directions: Have children color, cut out, and glue the boy together on another piece of paper. Older children can print the body part words around the boy. Encourage younger children to name the body parts as they put the boy together.

Draw a Person Game

Copy both the word cards and photo cards found on pages 66 to 72. Children who are learning to read the vocabulary in this unit can play with the word cards. Children who are not yet reading can play using the photo cards. Divide the children into two teams. Each team should have space to draw, either on the chalkboard or on a large piece of paper.

Place the word cards and photo cards facedown in separate piles. Team members take turns picking one card at a time and drawing that body part on the piece of paper or on the chalkboard. The first team to finish its drawing of a whole person is the winner.

This game is actually much more difficult than it may appear. The paper is blank. The first word or photo may be *eyebrow*. That body part must be drawn before another card is turned over. The second card might be *foot*. This takes some planning and an awareness of where to place the body parts on this large space. There will be lots of giggles and some very funny drawings. This activity is also wonderful for encouraging lots of oral language!

ankle	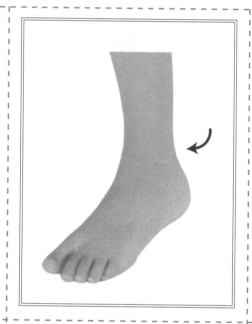	arm
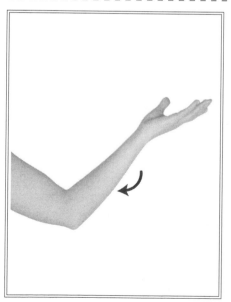	back	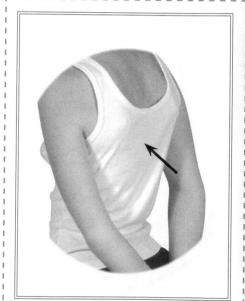

cheek		chest
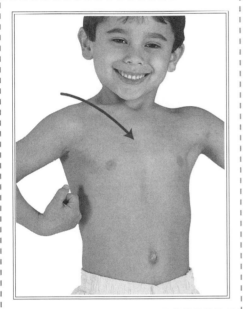	chin	
ear	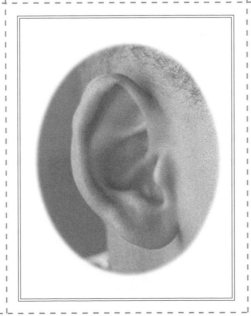	elbow

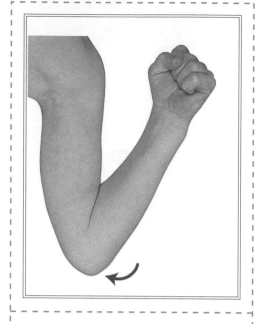

eye

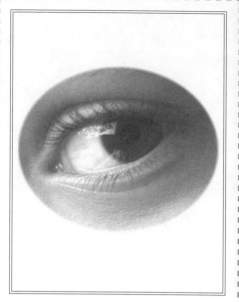

eyebrow

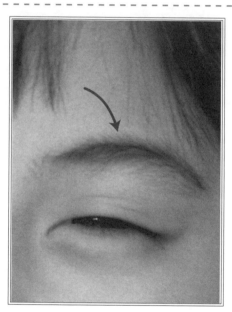

feet

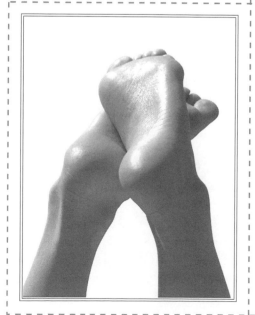

fingers

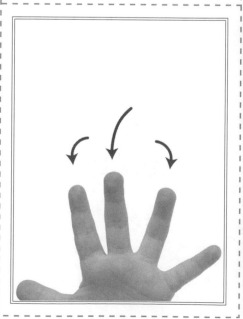

forehead

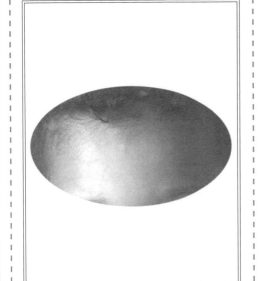

hair

hand

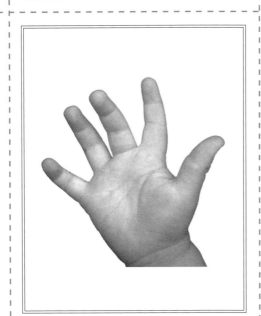

head

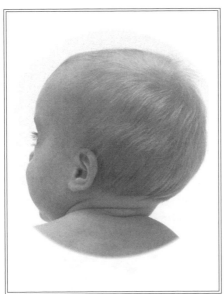

hips

knee

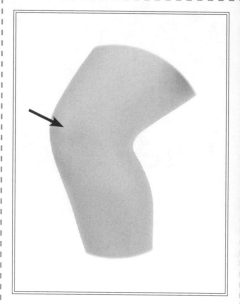

leg

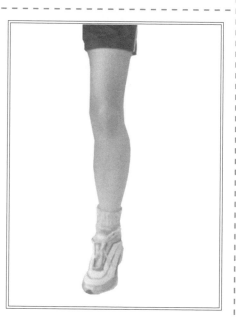

lips

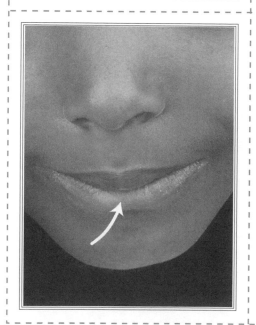

mouth

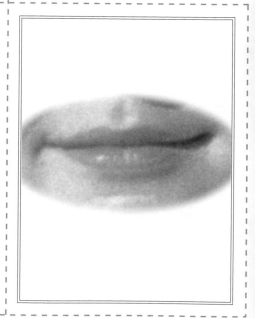

neck

nose

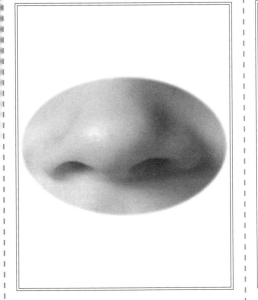

shoulder

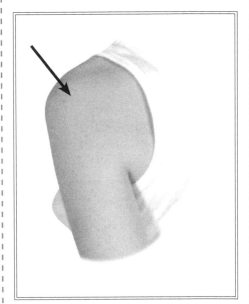

stomach

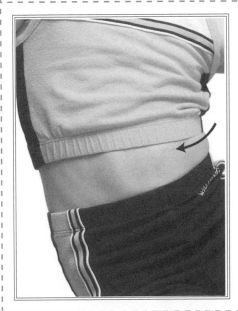

teeth

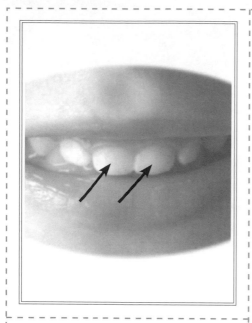

thumb

toes

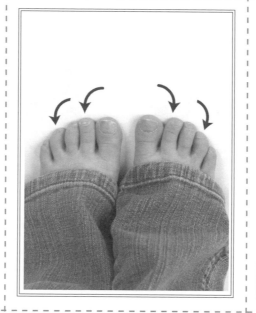

tongue

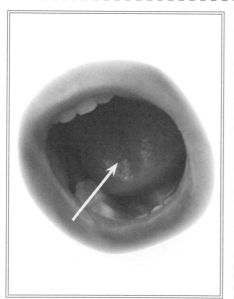

wrist

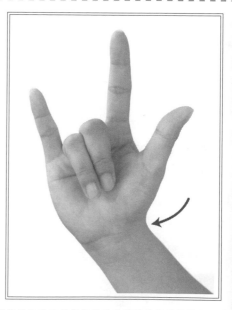

Unit 4: Clothes

Introduction

Clothing vocabulary is helpful for children to learn. We may wear similar kinds of clothes, but often there are a variety of names for one item, such as slacks, pants, trousers, blue jeans, jeans, leggings, capris, cargo pants, shorts—all of these are kinds of pants that people wear. There are many fun activities that will help children learn the names of clothing.

Copy two sets of the photo cards on pages 76 to 79 and let children match the pairs of pictures to introduce this new vocabulary.

Classroom Fashion Show

Have each student stand up one at a time and model what he or she is wearing. Describe the child's clothes first and then let the children try to explain what the child is wearing. Use this activity to introduce present continuous for descriptions, such as *he is wearing . . . , she is wearing . . . ,* and *they are wearing . . .*

Learning Words from Real Laundry

Hang up a clothesline in your classroom. Have a basket of clothing and clothespins ready. Invite children to come forward, pick up an article of clothing, tell the class the name of the clothing, and then hang it up on the clothesline.

Variation: For younger children, adapt this to be a receptive language activity. Hang many different articles of clothing on the clothesline. Ask students one at a time to come up and remove the piece of clothing you designate, such as, "Take down the green shirt," etc.

Describe "What You Are Wearing" Game

This is a fun game that children eagerly want to play. First, divide the class into two teams. Have one student from each team step outside of the classroom (only for a moment). Each team then chooses one person that they will describe. The two students return to the classroom, and the two teams take turns describing the team's chosen person. The first student to correctly guess which student is being described wins a point for the team.

Fashion Designers

Ask parents to send a pillowcase to school for their child. Carefully cut armholes, a slit up the front, and an opening for the child's head (see illustration). Using fabric crayons, fabric paint or puff paint, and by gluing on sequins or other adornments, children can turn their pillowcases into fancy new coats, shirts, or dresses. This activity can also be done with brown grocery bags.

Create Matching Visors

Children love to wear visors, and they are easy to make. You will need a paper plate and a half for each child. Have each child color and decorate the half paper plate and the edges of the whole paper plate. Once the pieces are completed, cut off the rim of the whole plate so that it is approximately 1.5" (4 cm) wide. Staple the half plate to the rim of the other plate (see illustration). Cover the staples with masking tape to protect the child's head. Then, measure the visors to the children's heads to ensure that they fit and tape the ends together.

❖◆❖

Dress-Up Extravaganza

The most effective way to teach children the names of specific clothing items is to name the articles of clothing as children are playing. Encourage parents to donate clothing that can be placed in a dress-up box. Garage sales are also a great source of clothing. Here is a list of essentials for your dress-up corner: dresses, skirts, blouses, hats, purses, high heels, slacks, shirts, nightgowns, pajamas, robes, slippers, shoes, jackets, boots, belts, jewelry, sport coats, athletic shirts, gowns, aprons, and even wigs.

Play Department Store

Use the dress-up clothing for imaginary shopping. Organize the clothes and have children ask for specific items. Provide a cash register and pretend money and keep shopping bags handy!

Paper Dolls

Girls especially love to play with paper dolls. Paper dolls can be purchased inexpensively at many large discount stores. Have children name the pieces of clothing as the dolls are being dressed.

Weather Bear

Purchase a commercially published "Weather Bear" bulletin board set or create one of your own. Attach one side of a piece of self-stick Velcro® to the bear and the corresponding piece to an article of clothing. Each morning, your students can dress the bear appropriately for the weather. Repeat out loud the names of the pieces of clothing as children place them on the bear. A large stuffed animal can also be used as a classroom weather mascot. Give the weather animal a special place in the classroom and dress it in real children's clothing.

What Is in the Closet? Game and Individual Activity (Page 75)

Individual activity: Reproduce page 75 for each child. Children can color and cut out the articles of clothing and then glue each piece in the correct section of the closet.

Prepare the game: Give each child a copy of page 75. The closet will become each child's individual game board and the articles of clothing will be the game pieces. Have children color their closets and the eight articles of clothing. Then, they should cut out all of the clothing game pieces and give the pieces back to you. Put all of the pieces of clothing in a bowl.

How to play: Invite several children at a time to come up to the bowl, close their eyes, and take eight pieces of clothing out of the bowl. Once all of the children have drawn eight clothing pictures, they should return to their seats and attempt to arrange the pieces of clothing in their closets. Two identical pieces may not be used; any duplicate clothing pictures must be set aside.

Then, have the children walk around and trade clothing pieces. For example, a child may say, "I will trade you my extra belt for the socks I am missing." Everyone wins this game! All of the closets will be full, the children will have socially interacted with each other, and they will have practiced using the vocabulary they are learning.

I Will Look Great

(sung to the tune of "The Wheels on the Bus")
What shall I wear to school today,
School today,
School today?
What shall I wear to school today?
I know what to wear!

I'll wear my jeans to school today,
School today,
School today.
I'll wear my jeans to school today,
And I will look GREAT!

(Continue the song with new items of clothing for each verse: I'll wear my belt . . . , my hat . . . , my shirt . . . , etc.)

What Is in the Closet?

(Directions found on page 74.)

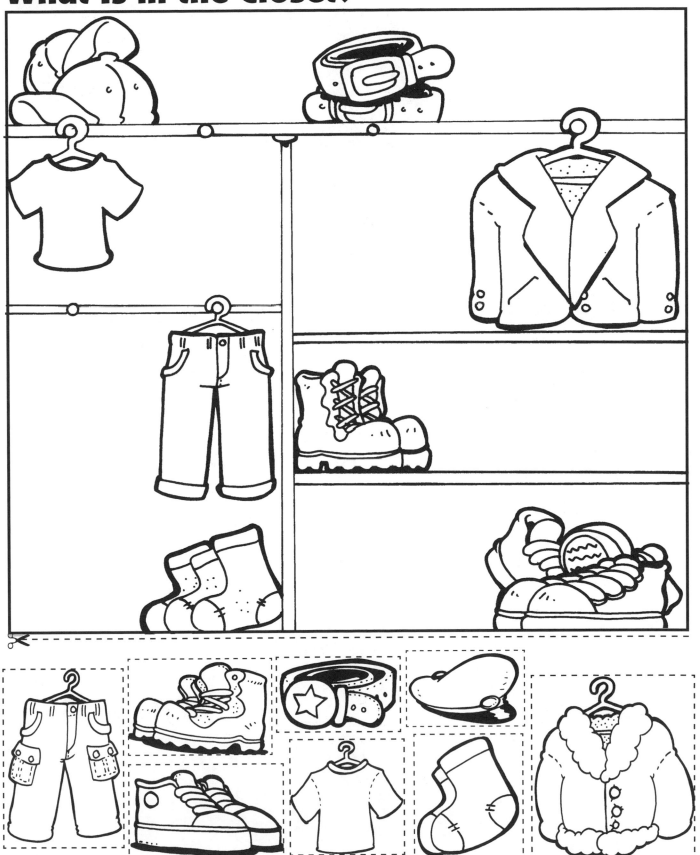

belt

boots

cap

dress

eyeglasses

hat

jacket

jeans

pajamas

pants		purse
	shirt	
shoes		socks

sweatshirt

sweater

T-shirt

underwear

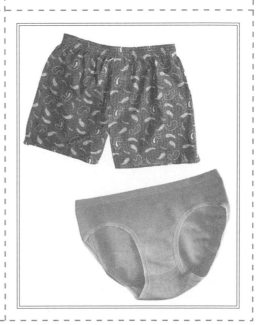

Unit 5: Colors

Introduction

Color words are among the first adjectives that children learn. While using crayons, play dough, and paint, children are hearing and learning these descriptive words.

A good way to introduce color words to young children is to tape several large pieces of white paper on a wall or chalkboard at the children's eye level. Model the activity for children by coloring on one of the white pieces of paper with a red crayon and saying, "Red." Next, color on another piece of paper with a blue crayon and say, "Blue."

Then, hand a red crayon to a student, ask her to color on the paper with red, and say, "Red." Continue until all of the children have had a chance to color with either red or blue on the correct papers. Repeat for several days until all of the colors have been introduced and practiced.

Musical Colors

Cut out construction paper circles in a variety of colors, one circle for each student. Lay the colorful paper circles in a large circle on the floor and have the children form a circle around them. Play some music and have children walk around the circle. When the music stops, children should stop, pick up the colorful paper circles that are closest to them, and name the colors they are holding.

Variation: When the music stops, children hold up their colorful paper circles and then group themselves with other children who are holding the same color circles.

Mixing Colors

Place shaving cream in resealable plastic bags. Add two (or more) colors of food coloring to the bags, seal them tightly, and watch the colors turn into new colors. Mix red and blue to discover purple, mix yellow and red to discover orange, and mix blue and yellow to discover green. Children love this. It is almost like magic!

Colorful Tin Cans

Ask parents to donate coffee cans. Paint each can a different color. Provide a wide variety of colorful objects for children to sort into the cans of the same color.

Color Big Book

Give each child a large piece of paper with a color word written at the top in the matching color. Children may either color a picture in the designated color or find and paste appropriately colored pictures on the page. Bind the pages together with yarn. Each day, have children add new color pages to the color big book.

Rainbow Writing

Most children really enjoy this activity. Provide each child with a page of shapes, letters, numbers, or designs or a card with the child's name on it. Have children trace over the images several times, each time using a different color of crayon. Ask children to identify the color each time a new crayon is chosen.

Crayon Rubbings

There are many different kinds of templates that can be commercially purchased. Place the template under a piece of paper and have the child rub a crayon on the paper over the template. A picture of the template's image will magically appear on the paper. Prepare your own templates by cutting shapes out of plastic lids such as margarine lids, coffee lids, or plastic bottles. Leaves, coins, and embossed greeting cards also work well as templates.

Colorful Cellophane

Colorful cellophane (purchased at card or craft stores) can create some exciting "color discoveries" for young children. Here is an assortment of activities that you can do with cellophane:

Decorate classroom windows. Colorful cellophane can be taped to window glass. Children will think it is fun to look through the window and see the world as red or blue or green. You can create a stained glass window by adding a new piece of cellophane to the window as you introduce each new color.

Overlap circles of color. Place pieces of cellophane in embroidery hoops. Children can look through the hoops or place different colors of hoops on top of each other to create new colors.

Create cardboard shape frames. Cut out frames of different geometric shapes from heavy cardboard. Tape cellophane along the back of each frame. These can be used in the same way as the embroidery hoop frames, but are not as expensive.

Look through cardboard spyglasses. Collect paper towel tubes and cover one end of each tube with cellophane. Children can pretend to be pirates and "spy" through the spyglasses.

Brown Bear, Brown Bear, What Do You See? Classroom Big Book

Brown Bear, Brown Bear, What Do You See? by Bill Martin Jr. and Eric Carle (Henry Holt ©1996) is one of the best-loved children's books for teaching colors. As you read the book with children, have them say each color word.

Create your own classroom big book with different animals. Write the story together as a class. The children might come up with *Pink Pig, Pink Pig, What Do You See?* The following pages might have purple cats, white bats, green dogs, black mice, or orange ants. Once you have decided on ten animals and their colors, divide the children into ten groups. Each group will be responsible for drawing and coloring a page for the classroom book. Provide each group with a large sheet of poster board, pencils, and crayons. Make sure that each child has an opportunity to color a section of the group's page. When completed, punch holes along the left side of each page and tie them together to create a book.

Colorful World

(sung to the tune of "Jack and Jill")

Purple grapes and
Red, red roses,
Orange pumpkins too.
These are things
That we all like
That grow for me and you.

Gray rain clouds and
Yellow leaves,
Black nights, and cold white snow.
These are all
Parts of the year
That make the seasons go!

Big green trees and
Yellow sun,
And blue, blue skies above.
These are things
That make our world,
The world that we all love.

Colors

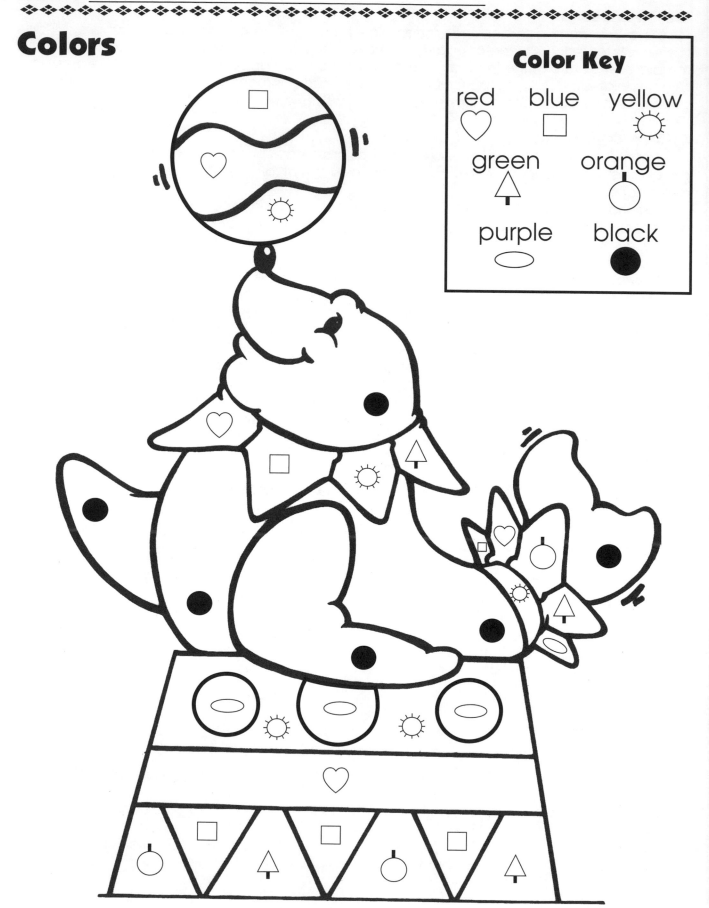

Color Key

red   blue   yellow

green   orange

purple   black

Match Colors

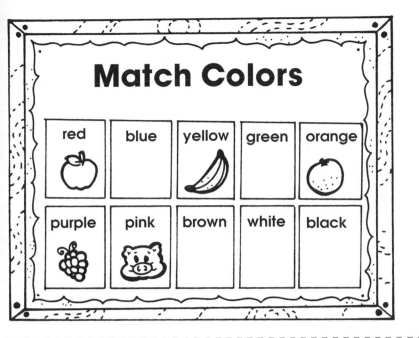

red	blue	yellow	green	orange
purple	pink	brown	white	black

Interactive Color Bulletin Board

Attach 9" x 12" (22.9 cm x 30.5 cm) pieces of felt in 10 different colors (red, blue, yellow, green, orange, purple, pink, brown, white, and black) to a bulletin board. Label each color. Then, find pictures that are predominately one of the featured colors. Laminate the pictures and attach the hook side of a piece of self-stick Velcro® to the back of each picture. The pictures will stick to the felt pieces on the bulletin board. Children will enjoy arranging all of the pictures and matching the colors of the pictures to the pieces of felt.

red

blue

yellow

green

orange

purple

white

black

brown

pink

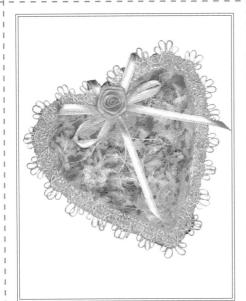

gray

tan

Unit 6: Community Helpers

Introduction
This unit could be divided by specific community helpers (for example, firefighter, police officer, and so on), which you could present to your students one person at a time. This is a great topic to incorporate picture books as well as field trips and special visitors to the classroom. Introduce the vocabulary by showing children the photos of the people found on pages 89 to 93.

Teachers: Help Us Learn
This activity is a fun "helper" to use as you begin the unit. Have children sit in a circle and talk about all of the things that teachers do for them. How do they think you have helped them? List the children's ideas on chart paper including all of the things that the children have learned so far this year. This conversation can also introduce additional vocabulary words such as *listen*, *share*, *clean up*, and *line up*.

Mail Carriers: I Sent a Letter
Have children dictate letters to you that they can send in the mail to their parents. The children can also include drawings with their letters. Encourage them to think up a lot to say by asking leading questions or providing sentence starters. Let children fold their letters and put the stamps on the envelopes. Older children who are more proficient in English may wish to print their own names and try to address the envelopes.

Mail Carriers: Let's Get Mail!
Have each child bring a shoe box to school. Children should decorate and print their names on their boxes. Provide the children with paper, envelopes, and stickers. Let them have the fun of "writing" at their own levels, putting the letters in envelopes, adding sticker stamps, and delivering their mail to their classroom friends.

Police Officer: Find My Child
This is a wonderful activity to build descriptive vocabulary. You will need a police officer's hat as a prop. Choose one child to play the role of the police officer. Have that child step outside of the room. Meanwhile, the class decides who is going to be "lost" and who is going to play the role of the parent. The parent then stands up, and the police officer is called in.

Dramatic play ensues:

Parent: "Oh, police officer, please find my child."

Police Officer: "Is the child a girl or a boy?"

Parent: "The child is a boy."

Police Officer: "What color is his shirt? What color are his eyes? What color is his hair?"

The parent must try to describe the child who is lost without looking at him, which would give the game away. The police officer tries to "find" the child by the simple description.

It is very important for newcomers to know what to do if they should get lost. Make a copy of the ID card (see right) for children to complete and carry with them.

My Name: _____

Address: _____

_____

Home Phone: _____

School Name: _____

School Phone: _____

Firefighters: Ladder on the Floor

Use masking tape to make a ladder on the floor. Have children walk with one foot on each side of the ladder or step from rung to rung. Then, challenge them to do this walking forwards, backwards, and on tiptoes. This activity increases balance without the danger of falling off a real ladder!

Firefighters: What Should You Do if . . .

Discuss with your class what they should do if:

❖ The child sees a fire down the street.
❖ The child sees another child playing with matches.
❖ The child smells smoke in her house.
❖ The child discovers that his own house is on fire.

Essential Vocabulary: 9-1-1 Emergencies

It is very important for all students to understand and learn the correct use of 9-1-1. Learning and practicing this procedure can greatly help if a real emergency ever occurs. Discuss the differences between what constitutes a "real" emergency and situations that do not warrant a 9-1-1 call. Have children practice calling 9-1-1 using a toy phone.

Community Helpers and Their Tools (Page 88)

Copy page 88 for each student. Ask students to color the page and then cut out the community helpers' tools at the bottom of the page. Children should then glue each tool to the correct community helper.

Miss Polly

This is a great rhythmic chant. Encourage students to tap their desks or clap their hands on the repeating words. After students are familiar with the storyline, invite volunteers to act out the chant while the rest of the class says the words.

Miss Polly had a dolly who was sick, sick, sick.
So, she called for the doctor to come quick, quick, quick.
The doctor came with his (her) bag and his (her) hat,
And he (she) knocked on the door with a rat-a-tat-tat.
He (she) looked at the dolly and he(she) shook his(her) head.
And he (she) said, "Miss Polly, put her straight to bed."
He (she) wrote on the paper for a pill, pill, pill.
"I'll be back in the morning with the bill, bill, bill."

Helper Song

(sung to the tune of
"A-Hunting We Will Go")

A teacher helps me learn,
A doctor makes me well,
A mail carrier brings the mail,
These helpers all are swell!

The police help keep us safe,
Janitors keep things clean,
A grocer sells our food to us,
These helpers all are keen!

A chef cooks up our food,
A waitress brings it out,
A dentist checks our teeth for us,
Let's give these folks a shout!

Firefighters save our homes,
A seamstress sews and mends,
Community workers are the best,
They are the best of friends!

Community Helpers and Their Tools (Directions found on page 87.)

Our Community

Community Helpers Book or Bulletin Board

Enlarge the photo cards on pages 89 to 93 and laminate them. Attach the photo cards of the people to a bulletin board or a poster board. Below each photo card, place the loop side of a piece of self-stick Velcro®. Place the hook side pieces of Velcro® on the backs of the photo cards of community helpers' tools. Let children match the tools to the people on the board.

business people

chef cook

construction worker

dentist

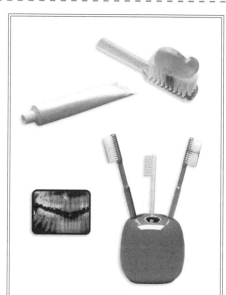

doctor

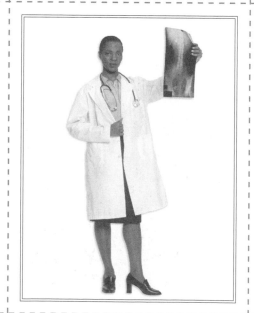

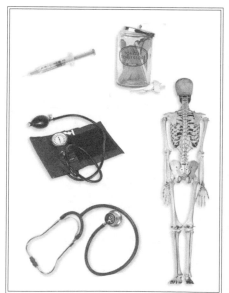

firefighter

grocer

janitor

mail carrier		
police officer		
seamstress		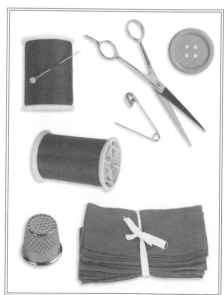

teachers

veterinarian

waitress & waiter

Table #7 Order

Unit 7: Emotions

Introduction

Copy the word and photo cards found on pages 97 to 99. Name and make the appropriate facial expression for each emotion. Ask students to model what you are doing. In addition to facial expressions, gestures can also help communicate feelings. Use the following examples to demonstrate various emotions.

Bored .... rest head on arm and sigh
Tired .... yawn and stretch
Sad................. frown and lower head
Proud .... stand tall with shoulders back
Angry .... clench teeth and squint eyes
Afraid .... shiver with eyes wide
Happy .... big smile
Confused....... scratch head
Noisy.............. cover ears
I like you......... hug or shake hands

Impatient..........look at pretend watch
Nervous.............tap feet or fingers
Bad smell ....hold nose
Good job..........thumbs up!
May I talk?........raise hand
Hello ....wave hand
Good-bye ....wave hand
Stop that...........hand up, palm facing out
Disgusted..........hands on hips, tap foot

Emotion Charades

Copy the word and photo cards found on pages 97 to 99. Turn the cards facedown. Have one student pick up a card and pantomime the emotion while the other children try to guess the emotion. The student who guesses correctly gets to keep the card and be the next player to pick a card to pantomime. The player with the most cards at the end of the game wins.

Variation: This game can also be played in two teams. One team member picks a card and then pantomimes the emotion to the rest of his team members for a specified amount of time. If the team guesses correctly within the given time period, they are awarded a point. If time runs out before a correct guess is made, that team does not receive any points and play is passed to the other team.

Mirror, Mirror on the Wall

Have children take turns making "emotional" faces in the mirror. Ask them what they think they look like when they are sad. What do they think they look like when they are happy? What do they think they look like when they are scared?

Ask children to choose partners and sit facing each other. One child should make a face that represents an emotion and the other child then names the emotion using a vocabulary word.

Classroom Emotion Book

Bring a digital camera to class. Take a variety of photos of the children. In each photograph, children should be showing a different emotion. Print the photographs on 8.5" x 11" (22 cm x 28 cm) paper and place them in plastic sheet protectors. Combine all of the photographs in a three-ring binder to create a classroom scrapbook of emotions. The children will enjoy looking at the book and practicing the vocabulary words for all of the emotions.

Quick, How Do You Feel? (Page 96)

Copy the "How Do You Feel?" face patterns found on page 96 for each child. Have children color the faces, cut them out, and tape them to craft sticks. Children should lay their four faces faceup in front of them. Then, act out or describe each situation listed below. Children should quickly choose and hold up the facial expression that matches the emotion they would feel during the described situation.

❖ You have to wait a whole hour for your brother at the bus stop. *(angry)*
❖ Your mom gives you a big hug. *(happy)*
❖ Your brother hits you for no reason. *(angry)*
❖ You get to buy some candy at the store. *(happy)*
❖ You and your best friend have a fight. *(sad)*
❖ There is a thunderstorm at night and the lights go out. *(scared)*
❖ Your best friend is moving away. *(sad)*
❖ Your friend gives you a birthday gift. *(happy)*
❖ Accidentally, you run into your friend in the hall, and he falls down. *(sad)*
❖ Your sister breaks your new toy. *(angry)*
❖ You get a special sticker on your school work. *(happy)*
❖ It is your first day at a new school. *(scared)*

If You're Happy and You Know It

If you're happy and you know it, clap your hands *(clap-clap)*
If you're happy and you know it, clap your hands *(clap-clap)*
If you're happy and you know it, then your face will surely show it
If you're happy and you know it, clap your hands. *(clap-clap)*
If you're happy and you know it, stomp your feet *(stomp-stomp)*
If you're happy and you know it, stomp your feet *(stomp-stomp)*
If you're happy and you know it, then your face will surely show it
If you're happy and you know it, stomp your feet. *(stomp-stomp)*
If you're happy and you know it, shout, "Hurray!" *(hoo-ray!)*
If you're happy and you know it, shout, "Hurray!" *(hoo-ray!)*
If you're happy and you know it, then your face will surely show it
If you're happy and you know it, shout "Hurray!" *(hoo-ray!)*
If you're happy and you know it, do all three *(clap-clap, stomp-stomp, hoo-ray!)*
If you're happy and you know it, do all three *(clap-clap, stomp-stomp, hoo-ray!)*
If you're happy and you know it, then your face will surely show it
If you're happy and you know it, do all three. *(clap-clap, stomp-stomp, hoo-ray!)*

When I Feel . . .

(sung to the tune of "Lullaby and Goodnight")
When I feel angry, I stamp my feet,
When I feel bored, I sigh.
When I feel happy, I joke and laugh,
When I feel sad, I cry.

When I feel scared, I want to hide,
When I feel strong, I leap!
When I feel silly, I dance around,
When I feel tired, I sleep.

How Do You Feel? Face Patterns

(Directions found on page 95.)

How Do You Feel?
Bulletin Board

Create a bulletin board with the labels *happy*, *sad*, *angry*, and *scared*. The face patterns on page 96 can also be used to label the bulletin board. Then, take a photograph of each child and print the child's name on the bottom of the photo. Children may pin their pictures under the faces that represent how they feel.

angry

bored

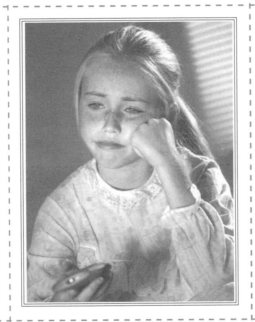

excited

grouchy

happy

loving

sad

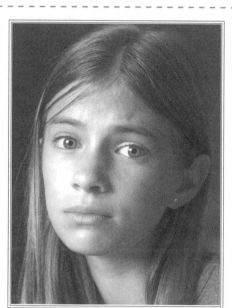

scared

serious

shy

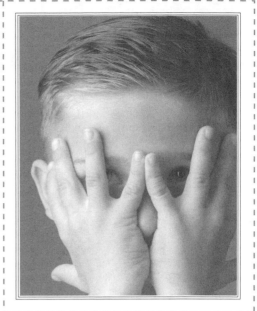

silly

surprised

tired

Unit 8: Family and Friends

Introduction

Before beginning this unit, ask the children's families to send a family photograph to school. If that is not possible, have children draw pictures of their families. Be sure to have your own family photo to share. Tell children about your family. Point out your mom, dad, grandparents, aunts, uncles, and siblings. Then, ask students to talk about the people in their photos or drawings. Have children describe the people using "family" vocabulary. Encourage children to tell something specific about each person, for example, how old the person is, what the person's job is, or an explanation of the person's hobbies or special interests.

Display the photos or drawings on a bulletin board labeled "Our Families."

Who Lives at My House?

Using a dollhouse and a variety of dolls, begin a discussion of home and the people that live there. Let each child have a turn placing all of her family members in the house. Do not forget to provide dolls that can represent grandparents, other relatives or friends, and pets. Who in the child's family is the tallest? Shortest? Youngest? Oldest?

My Family's Pet

Pets can become important members of a family. However, many young newcomers do not have the opportunity to own a pet. Make a predictable chart to model the reading process. The following is an example for a chart titled "The Pet I Want."

- ❖ I want a pet cat. *(child's name)*
- ❖ I want a pet dog. *(child's name)*
- ❖ I want a pet horse. *(child's name)*
- ❖ I want a pet fish. *(child's name)*
- ❖ I want a pet rabbit. *(child's name)*
- ❖ I want a pet snake. *(child's name)*

This is also a fun topic for a classroom big book. Children can draw their ideas of a good pet and print the sentence, "I want a pet _____," below their pictures. Bind all of the pages together to make a classroom book.

Favorite Family Songs

Ask children about the songs their families sing or listen to at home. Take turns singing some of the favorite songs of each child's family. Often these songs will be sung in the child's native language. You might also ask parents to volunteer to come to class and teach a song in their native language. This is a nice way for children to share something about their cultures and for children to learn to appreciate cultures different from their own.

Draw a Friend

Talk about friendship. What makes a good friend? Discuss how people make friends. Brainstorm a list of activities that friends do together. Then, ask children to go and sit next to a friend. Be sensitive about children who are new to class or children who are shy. Help those children to find and sit with another child that you know is friendly and welcoming.

Tell the pairs of friends they will take turns drawing pictures of each other. When the pictures are complete, print under each, "This is my friend _____." Then, ask each child to say one or two phrases or sentences that describe the friend.

This is my friend Jaily.

Friendship Cards for Everyone

This activity is designed to build vocabulary around the topic of friends. Write the title "Friends" on the chalkboard and then write a variety of words that would be used to describe a friend, such as *fun, play, share, good,* and *kind.* Also, include a few words that would not be used to describe a friend, such as *mean, hurt,* or *bad.* The children should decide together which words would not describe a friend.

Give each child a piece of colored construction paper. Show them how to fold the paper in half to make a card. Ask children to print one of the above "friend" words on their cards and decorate them. The children can then exchange their cards with another friend.

Who Is Missing?

Obtain a variety of dolls or use pictures of people for this activity. Label each person with a family name, such as "This is Mom," "This is Dad," "This is Uncle Joe," "This is Grandpa," etc. Place four or five of the dolls on a chalkboard ledge and show them to the children. Then, have the children close their eyes. While their eyes are closed, remove one doll. Ask children to guess who is missing.

My Family Tree (Page 102)

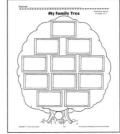

Make a copy of page 102 for each child. Have children draw pictures of various family members in the spaces on the tree. Print the person's name or relationship to the child (*Mom, Dad,* etc.) below each picture.

Playmate

Playmate, come out and play with me
And bring your dollies three.
Come climb my apple tree,
Play on my rain barrel,
Slide down my cellar door,
And we'll be jolly friends forever more.

Playmate, I cannot play with you,
My dollies have the flu,
Boo-hoo hoo hoo hoo hoo.
Can't play on your rain barrel or
Slide down your cellar door,
But we'll be jolly friends forever more.

Partner clapping pattern for "Playmate"

1. Clap own hands together.
2. Clap both hands against the partner's hands.
3. Clap own hands together.
4. Clap right hand with the partner's right hand.
5. Clap own hands together.
6. Clap left hand with the partner's left hand.

We Make a Family

(sung to the tune of "Twinkle, Twinkle Little Star"*)*

My brothers and sisters play all day,
There's a baby on the way,
With Mom and Dad, now look and see—
Together, we make a family!

My aunt and uncle come to call,
With cousins, we all have a ball.
We run and joke and laugh with glee—
Together, we make a family!

My grandmother makes us clothes to wear,
My grandfather hugs us like a bear.
They are in our family tree—
Together, we make a family!

Name_____

My Family Tree

(Directions found on page 101.)

Make a Family

Copy the word and photo cards on pages 103 to 107. Let children have fun arranging the photos into family groups. Encourage them to use their new vocabulary (mom, dad, grandpa, etc.) as they create the families. There are no right or wrong family groupings.

The photos represent diverse people and, when arranged into familial groups, can show some wonderful family diversity.

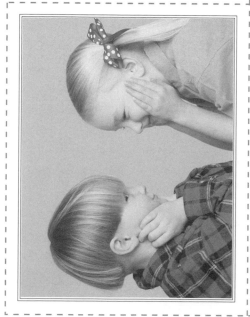
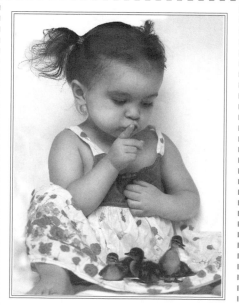

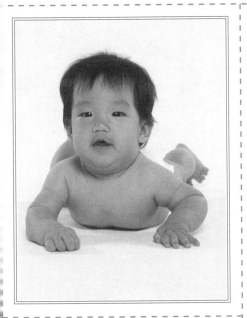

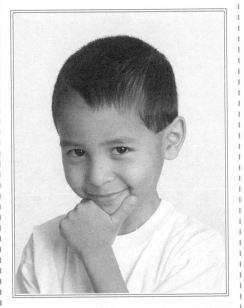

Family Word Cards

baby	sister	daughter
mom	mother	grandmother
grandma	granddaughter	aunt
son	brother	father
dad	grandfather	grandpa
grandson	uncle	cousin
family	friends	pets

Unit 9: The Farm

Introduction to Animals and Animal Sounds

All children seem to love animals and learning the names of the animals is always a lot of fun! Copy the word and photo cards found on pages 111 to 113. Have children work with partners. Distribute the cards to each pair. One partner should draw an animal card and give simple clues about the animal on the chosen card. The other partner must guess what the animal is.

Clothespin Animal Farm

This art project will last three days. You will need spring-type clothespins that clamp and farm animal-shaped cutouts that do not have legs. The clothespins will be the animals' legs (see illustration); when the animals are completed, they will stand alone.

Day 1: Students will paint one side of the clothespins and animal shapes and carefully place them to dry on the unpainted sides.

Day 2: Students will finish painting the other side of the animal shapes and clothespins and allow them to dry.

Day 3: Students should add details to the animal shapes and clip on the clothespin legs.

It is fun to have each child in your room create a different animal. When all of the farm animals are completed, make a barn and fences and arrange the animals in a farm scene.

Food from the Farm

Read the following paragraphs about the farmer's garden. Children may wish to pantomime all of the actions in the story as you read it.

The Farmer's Story

Farmer Brown plants seeds in his garden. He plants carrots, corn, and beans. When the vegetables are ready to harvest, he pulls them out of the ground or picks them off the plants. He loads them into his truck and takes them to the grocery store where he sells them.

Our mother buys these good, fresh foods at the store and brings them home. She washes them, cooks them, and serves them to us. "Yum, yum," we say, "these taste good!"

Next, have children go through grocery advertisements in the newspaper and cut out all of the foods that come directly from the farm. Cover a bulletin board with paper and let children fill it with all of the food pictures to make a garden collage.

Sprouting Seeds

Use many different receptacles to make your sprouting experiments interesting, such as tin cans, milk cartons, wax cups, eggshells in egg cartons, orange or grapefruit shells cut in half, muffin tins, jars, or glasses. An inverted Pyrex® bowl may be used as a protective cover at first.

Here are two methods for sprouting seeds:

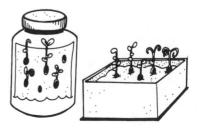

Jar method: Line a round jar or glass with blotting paper. Slip seeds between the glass and paper. Add 0.5 " (1.3 cm) of water.

Sponge method: Place a sponge in any flat shallow pan. Arrange seeds on it and cover them with a second sponge. Keep moist until the sprouting is quite developed. Large seeds, like lima beans, are easily observed. However, try untreated birdseed for interesting results.

Animal Guessing Games

Give children the following clues to see if they can discover which animal you are describing. Then, invite children to come up with their own clues for the animals.

1. I love the mud and have a curly tail. *(pig)*
2. I am very large and love to eat grass. I can give people all sorts of good food—especially ice cream. *(cow)*
3. People like to ride me. I am large and can help work on the farm. *(horse)*
4. I like to swim. Water seems to just run off my back. My mouth is called a bill. *(duck)*
5. I help people stay warm. I am very soft. *(sheep)*
6. I sit on a nest for long periods of time. I cluck. I have feathers. *(chicken)*

Animal Sounds Guessing Game

Before playing the game, review all of the sounds that farm animals make. Have children take turns making animal sounds and letting the other children guess which animal makes each sound. Children will also enjoy making their own animal sounds tape recording.

Three Little Ducks

This is a popular song to tie in with your farm unit. It is fun to perform this song using rubber ducks for props, finger movements, or actions.

Three little ducks went out waddling one day
Over the hill and far away.
Mother Duck said, "QUACK, QUACK, QUACK."
Only two little ducks came waddling back.
Two little ducks went out waddling one day
Over the hill and far away.
Mother Duck said, "QUACK, QUACK, QUACK."
Only one little duck came waddling back.

One little duck went out waddling one day
Over the hill and far away.
Mother Duck said, "QUACK, QUACK, QUACK."
Now, no little ducks came waddling back.
Zero little ducks went out waddling one day
Over the hill and far away.
Mother Duck said, "QUACK, QUACK, QUACK."
All three little ducks came waddling back.

The Farmer in the Dell

The farmer in the dell
The farmer in the dell
Hi-ho, the derry-o
The farmer in the dell

The farmer takes a wife
The farmer takes a wife
Hi-ho, the derry-o
The farmer takes a wife

The wife takes a child
The wife takes a child
Hi-ho, the derry-o
The wife takes a child

The child takes a nurse
The child takes a nurse
Hi-ho, the derry-o
The child takes a nurse

The nurse takes a cow
The nurse takes a cow
Hi-ho, the derry-o
The nurse takes a cow

The cow takes a dog
The cow takes a dog
Hi-ho, the derry-o
The cow takes a dog

The dog takes a cat
The dog takes a cat
Hi-ho, the derry-o
The dog takes a cat

The cat takes a rat
The cat takes a rat
Hi-ho, the derry-o
The cat takes a rat

The rat takes the cheese
The rat takes the cheese
Hi-ho, the derry-o
The rat takes the cheese

The cheese stands alone
The cheese stands alone
Hi-ho, the derry-o
The cheese stands alone

On the Farm

(sung to the tune of
"The Itsy Bitsy Spider")
On the farm, we have cows,
And goats and chickens too!
See the sheep out in the field,
The foal that is brand new.
The ducks swim on the pond and
The cat naps in the barn.
All these animals love
Their home here on the farm!

Name _____

Who Lives on the Farm?

Directions: Have children color the farm scene and the animals, cut out the animals along the dotted lines, and glue each animal on the scene.

Name _____

Animal Cracker Fun

Give each child a small paper plate filled with animal crackers. (Be sure to save enough crackers in the box to ensure a clean snack for snack time.) Let children sort the crackers according to the type of animal. The animal crackers can also be glued on farm scenes which have been drawn and colored by the children.

barn

cat

chicken

cow

dog

duck

goat

horse

mouse

pig

rabbit

sheep

tractor

Unit 10: Five Senses

Introduction

The five senses is an excellent unit for introducing a wealth of descriptive vocabulary, for example, for the sense of sight: *see, look, light, dark, bright,* and *watch;* for the sense of smell: *good, bad, perfume, sweet,* and *strong;* for the sense of taste: *sweet, sour, spicy, hot, cold, salty, good,* and *bad;* for the sense of hearing: *loud, quiet, shout, whisper, high,* and *low;* and for the sense of touch: *hard, soft, rough, smooth, wet,* and *dry.*

Begin this unit by showing the children through gestures what they will be learning about.

❖ **Sight:** Point to your eyes and say, "Sight is a sense. Your eyes help you see." Hold up different objects for which children already know the vocabulary, such as an apple. Ask students to identify each object. Then, ask, "How did you know this is an apple?" Encourage the response, "We could see it."

❖ **Hearing:** Cup your ears and say, "Hearing is a sense. Your ears help you hear." Sing a song the children are familiar with. Ask, "What did you hear?" They will tell you the name of the song. Then, ask, "How did you know?" Encourage the response, "We could hear it."

❖ **Smell:** Sniff and say, "Smell is a sense. Your nose helps you smell." Have students smell some perfume. Then, ask, "What sense did you use?" Encourage the response, "We could smell it."

❖ **Touch:** Hold up your hand, rub your thumb and fingers together, and say, "Touch or feeling is a sense. Most of the time, you use your fingers and hands to touch." Pass around a piece of soft fabric such as velvet. Ask students to tell you how it feels. Children will respond with words like *soft, nice,* etc. Next, ask, "What sense did you use?" The children will respond, "We could feel it." Rub your arm and tell the children, "Your skin can feel, too." Ask students to close their eyes and then touch each student's arm so that they can feel that all skin has the sense of touch.

❖ **Taste:** Pretend to eat something and say, "Yummmm." Then, say, "Taste is a sense. Your tongue helps you taste what is in your mouth." Have students close their eyes. Then, give each student a small piece of candy. Ask a student to describe how it tastes. Then, ask, "What sense did you use?" Encourage the response, "We could taste it."

Sense of Sight

Activity 1: Place a selection of everyday objects on a tray. Make sure these are objects that are already in the children's vocabulary. Let the children look at the tray for about 15 seconds. Tell them to close their eyes, remove an object, and ask them to tell you which item is missing.

Activity 2: Show children another tray of objects. Remove the tray and have children work together to try to remember everything they saw on the tray.

Activity 3: You will need wet coffee filters for each child, several muffin tins filled with thinned paint or water with food coloring added, and eyedroppers. Have children drop a small amount of paint or colored water on the wet coffee filters. As more color is added, the colors will blend together to create new colors.

Sense of Touch

Activity 1: Place some small objects in a box and cover them with a towel. Each child will close his eyes, pick up one object, and then guess what the object is simply by feeling it.

Activity 2: Practice printing new vocabulary or reading words with the sense of touch. Fill cookie sheets with salt, sand, or rice. Let children print words on these texture trays.

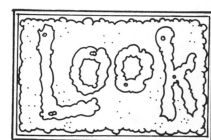

Sense of Smell

Activity 1: Provide each child with five 6" x 9" (15.24 cm x 22.9 cm) half pages of construction paper in the following colors: purple, red, orange, yellow, and green. On the **purple** paper, have children draw grapes. On the **red** paper, they should draw cherries. On the **orange** paper, they may draw an orange. On the **yellow** paper, children should draw two lemons. Finally, on the **green** paper, ask them to draw two limes. Then, have children paint slightly diluted white glue on each of their pages and immediately sprinkle the corresponding flavored gelatin on each picture. Allow the pages time to dry, bind them together into a small book, and then let children enjoy smelling each colorful page.

Activity 2: Bring in a variety of things that are safe for children to smell, such as coffee, popcorn, chocolate, bananas, oranges, peppermints, peanut butter, vinegar, perfume, onions, and bell peppers. Ask children to close their eyes and use their sense of smell to identify or describe each of the items.

Sense of Hearing

Activity 1: Make some musical instruments. Have each child decorate the bottoms of two paper plates. Add uncooked rice or pasta, dried beans, or small bells to one of the plates. Cover the rim of that plate with white glue, invert the second plate, and place it on top of the glued plate. Allow the glue to dry completely and reinforce the edges with tape. Let children shake their plates to make music, experimenting with different sounds, rhythms, and movements, such as loud, soft, noisy, quiet, fast, and slow.

Activity 2: Instruct children to close their eyes and listen carefully. Describe a scene using vocabulary that you know will be understood. Then, have them draw what they heard.

Activity 3: Make a tape recording of common, everyday sounds such as a dog barking, a ringing telephone, or a honking car horn. Have children identify the sounds. It is also fun to record each of the children's voices and let children guess who is talking.

Sense of Taste

Bring in a selection of foods that the children will be familiar with, for example apples, bananas, cheese, yogurt, pickles, etc. (Be sure to first inquire about possible food allergies and religious or other food preferences.) Give children the language they need to describe each food, such as *sweet, sour, salty, fruity,* etc. Children may also enjoy closing their eyes and trying to guess what foods they are eating.

Five Senses

(sung to the tune of "My Bonnie Lies Over the Ocean")
My fingers can feel and touch things,
My ears hear the wind in the trees,
My eyes see, my nose smells, my tongue tastes,
These all are my senses, you see!

Touch, taste, see, smell, hear the world all around,
See, smell, touch, hear, taste the good things that abound!

Name_____

Which Sense?

Directions: Have children color each picture and then cut out and glue the small pictures to the correct scenes.

Interactive Five Senses Bulletin Board

Enlarge and copy the five senses word and photo cards found on pages 117 to 118. Use them as headings on an interactive bulletin board. Cut out a large variety of pictures from magazines. Children may sort and then glue the pictures under each of the headings. Many of the pictures could be placed under more than one sense. Encourage children to talk about their placement choices.

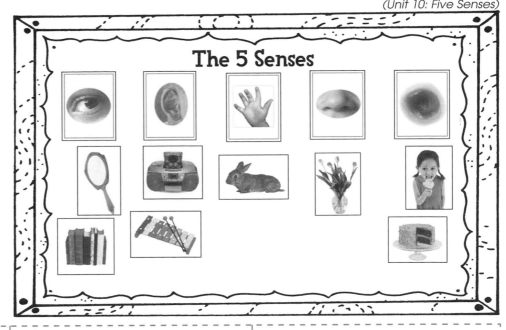

The 5 Senses

see

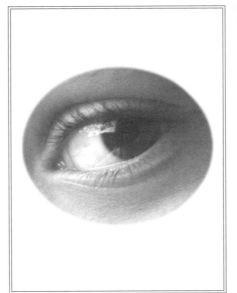

hear

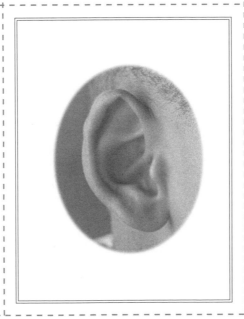

taste

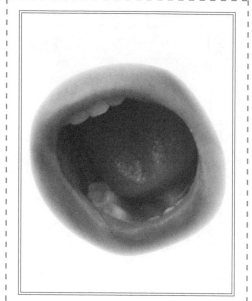

touch

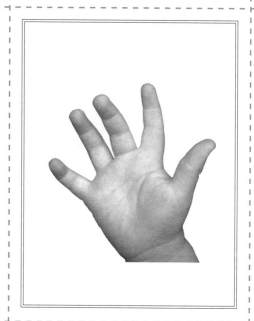

smell

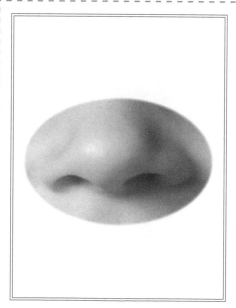

Unit 11: Food

Introduction

Children will learn the names of over 55 different foods in this unit. This unit can also provide opportunities to use the following vocabulary and grammatical structures:

- ❖ Do you like . . .?
- ❖ I like it.
- ❖ Yes, I do.
- ❖ I don't like it.
- ❖ No, I don't.
- ❖ What do you like?

Copy the word and photo cards found on pages 122 to 134 on card stock. Choose which cards you will show the children, only introducing as many as you think your class is ready to learn.

Pick up a photo card, say the name of the food, and with a huge smile say, "I like it." Then, ask a student, "Do you like it?" Encourage the response, "Yes, I do." Repeat until all students understand the meaning of these two phrases.

Next, pick up another photo card, say the name of the food, make a disgusted face, and say, "I don't like it." Then, ask another student, "Do you like it?" Encourage the response, "No, I don't." Once again, repeat until all students understand the meaning.

When learning the new food vocabulary, encourage conversations such as, "Do you like cookies?" "Yes, I like cookies." Do you like radishes?" "No, I don't like radishes." "What do you like?" "I like celery."

Vegetable Stew

Gardens grow so many wonderful vegetables! Let students make lunch using a variety of healthy and good tasting vegetables and this easy recipe.

- ❖ 2 pounds ground beef (may be precooked)
- ❖ 1 onion, diced (optional)
- ❖ 6 potatoes, peeled and diced
- ❖ 6 carrots, peeled and diced
- ❖ 1 can green beans (or 1/2 pound fresh)
- ❖ 1 can whole-kernel corn (or fresh from 3 ears of corn)
- ❖ 1 15-ounce can tomato sauce
- ❖ 4 cups water
- ❖ 1 teaspoon salt
- ❖ 1/2 teaspoon pepper
- ❖ dash of oregano

Brown the ground beef and onions; drain. Add the remaining ingredients. Cook on medium heat for 20 minutes and simmer for 30 additional minutes. (Increase cooking time if fresh green beans are used.) Makes 12 servings.

Special Note: Before completing any food activity, ask families' permission and inquire about students' food allergies and religious or other food preferences.

Stamping with Food

Use a variety of foods to create stamps. Potatoes, carrots, celery, apples, and cucumbers all make excellent stamps. Cut an end from the food so that one of the surfaces is flat. Dip the food in a small pan of tempera paint and then press onto paper.

Our Own Grocery Store

Collect food containers, such as egg cartons; cereal, cracker, pudding, and cookie boxes; milk cartons or jugs; soup, vegetable, and fruit cans; margarine tubs; and juice cans. Wash and dry the containers and make sure the cans do not have any sharp edges. Let children arrange a classroom grocery store, complete with cash register, shopping carts, and brown paper bags. Encourage the use of food vocabulary as children plan their shopping trips, fill their carts, and make their purchases.

Sort by Food

Use the food photo cards (pages 122 to 134) copied on card stock for the unit's introduction. Have children sort the cards according to food type: fruit, vegetables, meats, breads, and dairy products. You may choose to add additional categories such as desserts, spices, fats, and drinks. Some foods may belong in more than one category; invite students to discuss their choices.

Make Your Own Pizza

Create a paper plate pizza topped with a variety of foods drawn or cut from magazines. Then, describe your pizza to the children: "I love pineapple, olives, cheese, tomatoes, and chicken on my pizza." Next, give each child a paper plate, construction paper, markers, scissors, glue, and magazines. Ask children to create their own favorite pizzas. Can students name each ingredient on the pizzas they have made?

Make a Shopping List

Using the advertisement section of the newspaper, have children cut out pictures of food and glue them on a sheet of paper. When they are finished, have children "read" their shopping lists to the class.

Let's Go Grocery Shopping! (Page 121)

Copy page 121 for each child and cut off the directions at the bottom of the page. The goal is for children to identify the names of some common foods and to follow oral directions. Read the directions, allowing plenty of time for students to complete each step.

Favorite Foods

(sung to the tune of "Mary Had a Little Lamb")
I like apples, they are sweet,
Water's cool,
Corn is, too!
Ice cream is my favorite treat,
I love these foods, I do!

Hamburgers just can't be beat
With carrots to crunch
For a lunch!
Tacos are so fun to eat,
All these foods taste great.

Salad is so good with fish,
Cake is neat,
I like meat!
Pancakes are my favorite dish,
All these foods are treats.

Tomatoes are so red and round,
I love fries
And apple pies!
Popcorn makes a popping sound,
You'll love these foods, just try!

Name _____

Let's Go Grocery Shopping!

Directions: Read the following directions to the students, allowing time to complete each step.

1. Draw an X on an **egg**.
2. Color the **watermelon** red.
3. Color a loaf of **bread** brown.
4. Color an **apple** red.
5. Color an **orange** orange.
6. Color the **cheese** yellow.
7. Draw a circle around a container of **milk**.
8. Color a jug of **juice** orange.
9. Color another jug of **juice** yellow.
10. Color the cans of **soda pop** any color you choose.

apple

bananas

beans

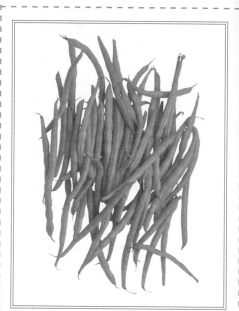

bread

breakfast

broccoli

butter

cake

carrots

cauliflower

celery

cereal

cheese

chicken fingers

chips

cookies

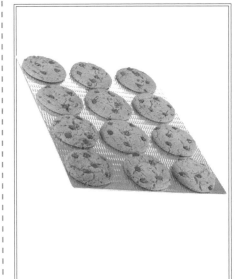

corn

crackers

dinner

doughnut

eggs

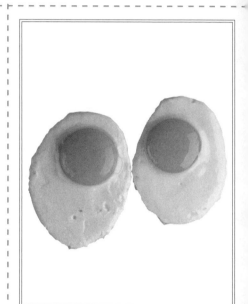

french
fries

grapefruit

grapes

grilled cheese sandwich

hamburger

hot dog

ice
cream

jello

lemonade

lunch

macaroni
&
cheese

milk

mustard
&
ketchup

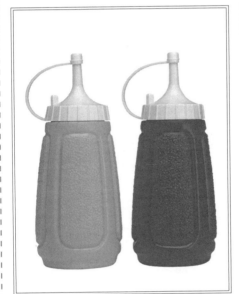

orange
juice

oranges

pancakes

peanut butter & jelly sandwich

pickle

pie

pineapple

pizza

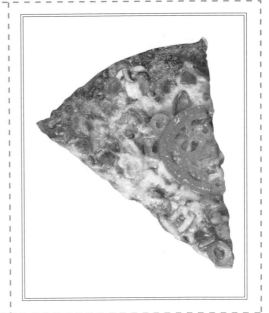

popcorn

popsicles

potato

pretzel

salad

salt
&
pepper

sandwich

soda
pop

spaghetti

strawberries

toast

taco

tomato
soup

water

watermelon

yogurt

Unit 12: Household Objects

Introduction
In this unit, children will learn the names of 54 common household objects, including names of furniture, kitchen and bathroom items, and other everyday objects. Copy the word and photo cards found on pages 138 to149 on card stock. Organize the cards into categories that make sense for your lesson plans and introduce one category at a time.

Pictionary
Copy the photo cards found on pages 138 to149 and place them in a container. Have a child choose, without looking, one card from the container. The child should then draw the item in the photo with chalk on the chalkboard. The first child to correctly guess the name of the object being drawn gets to be the next child to choose a card. It is also great fun to use clay to sculpt the object for students to guess.

Cut and Paste Fun
Tape two large pieces of paper on a wall or chalkboard. Tape a toothbrush to the first piece of paper and tape a plastic spoon to the second piece of paper. Ask students where these objects are usually found. Then, have children look through newspapers, magazines, and catalogs for pictures of other objects that belong in either the bathroom or the kitchen. Children should cut out those objects and tape or paste them on the correct pieces of paper.

Window Paint
To begin, use tape and newspaper to protect the walls and floor. Mix liquid dish washing soap into tempera paint to help make the paint removal easier. Then, let children create a window masterpiece. ***Special Note:*** The longer the window paint is left on a window, the harder it will be to remove. As an alternative, you can cover the window with cellophane and have children paint on the cellophane instead of the glass.

What's Behind the Door?
Read aloud *There's a Nightmare in My Closet* by Mercer Mayer (Dial, 1968). Children should pretend to open a closet door each time you read the word *closet*. After reading the story, have each child place glue along one long side of a piece of brown construction paper and then glue the paper onto a piece of white paper to make a door. Fold the brown paper back so that the door can open and close. Have children draw and color surprises behind their doors.

A Chair for My Mother
Read *A Chair for My Mother* by Vera B. Williams (Greenwillow, 1982). This heartwarming story is about a girl, her mother, and her grandmother who save their money to buy a big, comfortable chair after everything they own is lost in a fire. Have the children draw and color what they believe would be the world's best chair. What colors are the chairs? How big is each chair? Have students describe their chair drawings for their classmates.

Tabletop Painting

Cover the tabletop with finger painting paper. Make some instant pudding and let the children have fun finger painting with this yummy texture.

Dollhouses and Building Blocks

Playing with a dollhouse is an effective way to teach vocabulary because it provides children with concrete examples. Play with the children and model the vocabulary, for example, "Let's put the baby to bed. The boy can sit on the chair." If the boys are reluctant to play with the dollhouse, provide them with the experience of building furniture using blocks. Beds, chairs, sofas, tables, and many other pieces of furniture are easily constructed with blocks and a little imagination.

Hold a Furniture Building Contest

Have children work in teams. Provide a variety of small boxes, cardboard tubes, paper, and other art supplies or simply use blocks. Say the name of a piece of furniture and challenge the children to work together to construct it.

Play Hide and Seek

Close your eyes while the children hide. Each time you find a child, the child must describe where he was hiding, for example, by the chair, under the table, etc. This practice will build students' vocabulary and increase their understanding of positional concepts.

Photo Card Furniture Game

Reproduce the photo cards of furniture on pages 138 to 149 for each child. Have children lay the cards faceup in front of them. Say the name of a piece of furniture and have the children pick up that photo as fast as they can. Children love this game and it can be used with any of the themes presented in this book.

Variation: Reproduce one set of the photo cards of furniture on pages 138 to 149. Have children sit in a circle. Place the cards faceup in the middle of the circle so that everyone can see them. Have the children close their eyes and then remove or turn one card facedown. The first child to identify which card is gone receives a point. Increase the difficulty of the game by increasing the number of cards removed or turned facedown.

Hidden Household Objects (Page 137)

Copy page 137 for each child. Have children find and circle or color the 12 objects hidden in the house. Name the objects as you list them on the board for reference: *book, camera, comb, cup, eyeglasses, flashlight, fork, iron, keys, letter, toothbrush,* and *wallet.*

In My House

(sung to the tune of "Alouette")

In my bedroom,
There's my bed and bookshelves,
There's a chair there,
A clock, a desk, a phone.

In the kitchen, there's a stove,
A sink, a toaster, bread in loaves,
Cups, a broom!
Forks and spoons!

In the hallway,
There's a mirror and pictures,
And a rug that spells out
"Welcome Home."

On the porch,
We have a chair with pillows,
And a stool where
Dad puts up his feet.

The living room has our TV,
A table, sofa, books to read!
Flowers galore!
A swinging door!

My house is a place
Where friends can all meet,
A home where family
Eats and plays and sleeps.

Hidden Household Objects

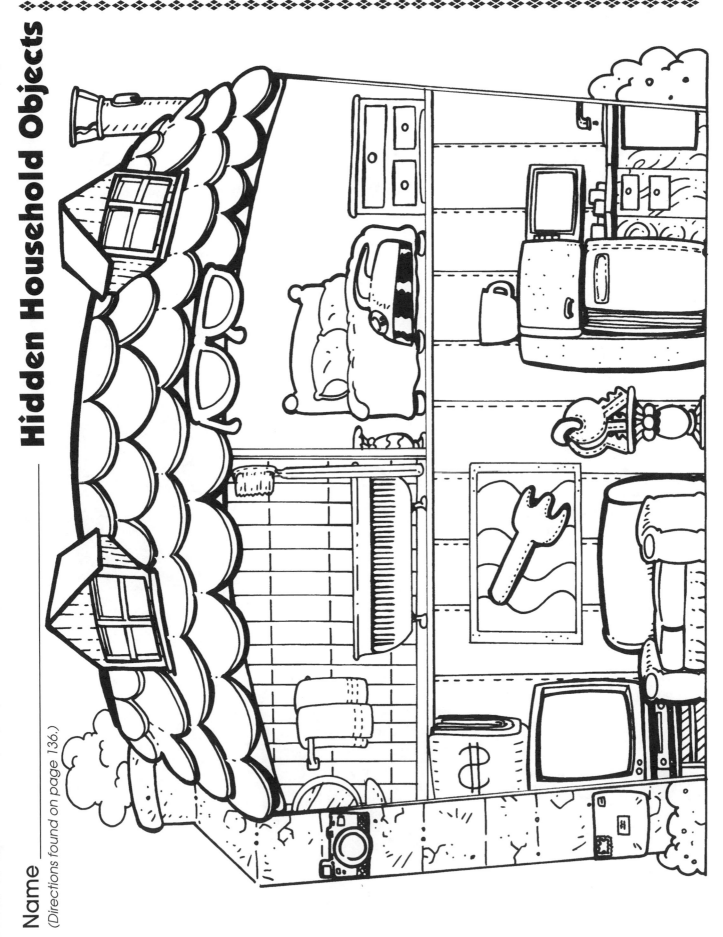

Name
(Directions found on page 136.)

bathtub

bed

books

bookshelf

bowls

broom

brush

camera

chair

clock

comb

cup

desk

door

fan

flashlight

flowers

fork

glass

hairdryer

house

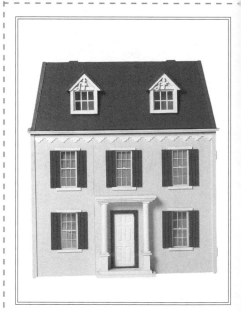

iron

ironing board

keys

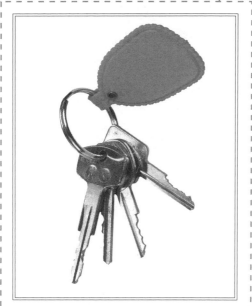

knife

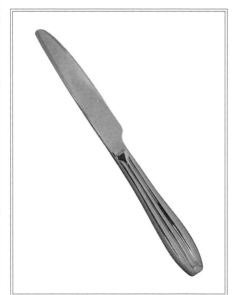

lamp

letter

mirror

pan

pillow

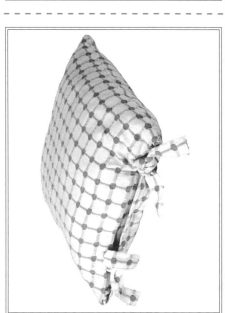

plate

refrigerator

rug

shampoo

shovel

shower

sink

soap

sofa

spoon

stool

stove

table

telephone

television

toaster

toilet

toilet paper

toothbrushes

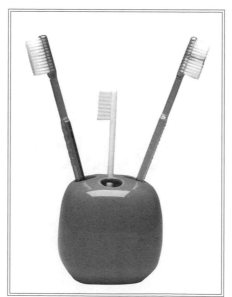

toothpaste

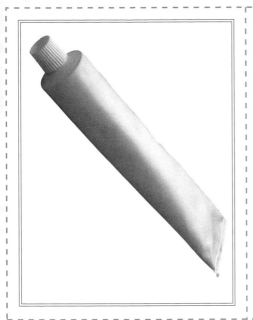

towels

vacuum

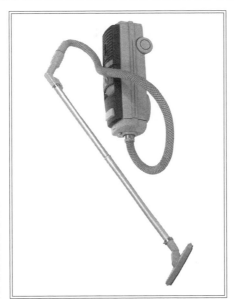

wallet

window

Unit 13: Manners

Introduction

One of the most difficult challenges for a student from another country is understanding a new culture and learning the culturally accepted rules for manners and social interaction. What may be perfectly acceptable behavior in one culture may be viewed as rude in another culture. Often, newcomers can unknowingly upset others or have their actions misinterpreted. These children need to learn manners and social skills quickly. It can be helpful to start with learning simple phrases and knowing when to use them. The following are some good phrases and guidelines that may be helpful:

Phrases to Be Learned

* Please.
* Thank you.
* I'm sorry.
* Excuse me.
* May I?
* You're welcome.
* Nice to meet you.

Guidelines to Good Manners

Social Skills
* Do not interrupt when someone else is speaking.
* Never spit.
* Do not burp or pass gas on purpose.
* Do not hit, push, or shove others.

Good Table Manners
* Eat after everyone is seated.
* Eat with proper utensils—not with a knife or your fingers.
* Use a napkin to wipe your mouth.
* Clear your dishes when you are done eating.
* Put your napkin in your lap.
* Chew with your mouth closed.
* Drink quietly—no gulping.

Good Hygiene
* Routinely take baths, brush teeth, and wash and comb your hair.
* Use a tissue to cover your mouth when you cough or sneeze.
* Wash hands before you eat and after using the restroom.

Good Social Behaviors
* Take turns.
* Wait for a turn.
* Pick up your toys.

Shopping to Practice Using "Please," "Thank You," and "You're Welcome"

Place plastic fruits and vegetables or the corresponding photo cards found on pages 122 to 134 in a shopping basket. Gather the students around you and encourage them to ask politely for what they want as you model responses, for example, "What do you want?" "An apple, please." "Here you are." "Thank you." "You're welcome." Then, call back the objects from the students, "Apple, please," and students respond by putting the items back into the basket.

Play Tea Party

Before you begin, you will need paper plates, napkins, forks, knives, spoons, and cups. Say, "Today, you are going to learn good table manners. *Table manners* means how you act while you are eating." Give each student one of the above items. Name the item and ask the student to repeat its name. Explain and model the Good Table Manners rules (above). Then, serve lemonade and cookies for actual manners practice.

Catch You Being Good

Create a "Magic Words" bulletin board. Cut out a magician's top hat from black construction paper for each child. Print the child's name on the brim. Each time you catch a child using one of the magic words, the child gets to put a sticker on the top hat. Send the hats home at the end of the week.

The Importance of Being Honest and Trustworthy

Discuss the word *honesty*. What does it mean to say we are honest? Use examples such as we tell the truth and do not lie, we respect the property of others, and we do not take things that do not belong to us.

Activity 1—Pinocchio: Read or tell the story of Pinocchio. This puppet has to earn the privilege of becoming a real boy and has many adventures. One of Pinocchio's biggest lessons is learning not to tell lies. Every time he lies his nose grows! For fun, use a puppet to help you tell Pinocchio's story.

Activity 2—George Washington: Our first president is also famous for being truthful. It is said that as a child he chopped down a cherry tree in his parents' yard and admitted the wrong, saying, "I cannot tell a lie. I chopped down the cherry tree." Bring in cherries for the children to sample. Ask children to discuss times they were honest and truthful with their parents.

Activity 3—The Boy Who Cried Wolf: This is another wonderful story that illustrates the bad things that can happen when someone tells a lie. Have children act out the story as you tell it. Let children draw a picture of a sheep to help them remember the story.

Good or Bad Manners (Page 152)

Copy page 152 for each child. Discuss what is happening in each box. If children think the scene is showing good manners, they should circle or color the smiling face. If they think the scene is showing poor manners, they should circle or color the frowning face.

Good Manners Game Reproducible Cards (Pages 153 and 154)

Copy the game cards found on pages 153 to 154, one set of cards for every group of three to four children. Read the cards with students and discuss each card's meaning.

Mix up the cards and place them facedown. Each child will take a turn to choose a card, read it (provide help as needed), and then decide if it shows good or poor manners. One point is scored for a good manners card; zero points are earned for a poor manners card. The player with the most points after all of the cards are drawn wins.

Best Behavior

(sung to the tune of "The Animal Fair")
I know how to act just right,
I never eat with a knife,
When my mouth is full, I never talk,
In halls, I don't run but walk!

In the bathroom, I wash my hands,
I pick up my toys—I can!
I don't spit or burp, and everyone knows
To use a tissue to blow your nose,
Your nose, your nose, your nose!

Magic Words

(sung to the tune of "A-Tisket, A-Tasket")
Say please and thank you,
To please the folks around you;
Say please for something that you want,
And then you say, "Why, thank you!"

Say may I, please, may I,
When you want to drop by,
Or if you want to go and play,
Always ask, "Please, may I?"

Name_____

Good or Bad Manners

(Directions found on page 151.)

You say, "Please."	You say, "Thank you."	You spit.
You use a tissue when you sneeze.	You chew with your mouth closed.	You burp.
You begin to eat after everyone sits down.	You make a mistake and say, "I'm sorry."	You ask, "May I?"
You eat with a knife.	You wash your hands before you eat.	You do not cover your mouth when you cough.

You use a napkin to wipe your mouth.	You meet a new person and say nothing.	You take turns.
You speak with your mouth full of food.	You put your napkin on your lap.	You interrupt when someone is talking.
You wipe your mouth on your sleeve.	You bump into someone and do not say, "Excuse me."	You wait your turn.
You gulp and drink loudly.	You pick up your toys.	You say, "You're welcome."

Unit 14: Numbers

Introduction

Numbers often are easy for young English language learners to grasp. There are many games, stories, rhymes, and songs that help children understand number concepts.

Activity 1—Texture Numbers: Copy the word and number cards found on pages 160 to 164 on heavy card stock. Trace each numeral with white glue, sprinkle it with sand or salt, and let it dry. When the glue is completely dry, children will be able to trace the numerals with their fingers and "feel" the number as they say each number word.

Activity 2—Button Set Cards: Make number cards that show sets by gluing buttons on card stock. For example, on one card glue one button, on the next card glue two buttons, and so on. The children can match a numeral card to the correct set on a button card.

Stand Up 10!

Have students sit in a circle and count from 1 to 10 by going around the circle. For example, the first child says "one," the next child says, "two," and so on. Each time, the student who calls out "10" must stand up and will no longer count. Continue until only one student is left sitting. For extra fun, try counting backwards or use numbers from 11 to 20 or numbers 20 to 30.

Make a Number Set

Play some music and have students walk, skip, jump, hop, etc., around the room. Stop the music and then call out a number between 1 and 10. The students must scramble, getting together to form a group or groups that equal the number that was called.

Beat the Clock

Hand out the numeral cards on pages 160 to 164, one card to each child. Time the students to see how quickly they can line up in numerical order. Let them do it again to see if they can beat their previous time. Then, have them exchange numbers and try again.

Clothespin Wheel Numbers 1 to 10

Print the numbers 1 to 10 around the edge of a paper plate and print the same numbers on spring-type wooden clothespins. The children can then attach the numbered clothespins next to the matching numbers on the plate, naming each number as they work.

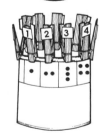

Clothespin Can Numbers

Draw sets of numbers along the top edge of a can (see illustration). If you cannot print directly on the can, draw the number sets on paper and then glue the paper to the can. You can also create number sets with stickers. Have children attach numbered wooden clothespins (see activity above) along the top of the can next to the corresponding sets of numbers.

Dominoes (Pages 158 and 159)

Copy pages 158 and 159, cut out the dominoes, and laminate them for durability. Pass five dominoes to each player and place the remaining dominoes facedown as a "bank." The first child puts any domino in the center; the next player must match one end of the first domino. If he cannot, he may take one from the bank. The first child to play all of her dominoes wins.

Songs and Rhymes about Numbers

Rhymes are one of the best ways to help young children learn to count and to practice number words. Teach children some of the following rhymes and encourage them to indicate the meaning of each number word by holding up the correct number of fingers or a number card. These rhymes will provide hours of educational fun!

Songs to Help Learn Numbers

This Old Man

This old man, he played one;
He played knick-knack on my thumb.
With a knick-knack paddywhack,
   give a dog a bone,
This old man came rolling home.

This old man, he played two;
He played knick-knack on my shoe.
With a knick-knack paddywhack,
   give a dog a bone,
This old man came rolling home.

This old man, he played three;
He played knick-knack on my knee.
With a knick-knack paddywhack,
   give a dog a bone,
This old man came rolling home.

This old man, he played four;
He played knick-knack on my door.
With a knick-knack paddywhack,
   give a dog a bone,
This old man came rolling home.

This old man, he played five;
He played knick-knack on my hive.
With a knick-knack paddywhack,
   give a dog a bone,
This old man came rolling home.

This old man, he played six;
He played knick-knack on my sticks.
With a knick-knack paddywhack,
   give a dog a bone,
This old man came rolling home.

This old man, he played seven;
He played knick-knack up in heaven.
With a knick-knack paddywhack,
   give a dog a bone,
This old man came rolling home.

This old man, he played eight;
He played knick-knack on my gate.
With a knick-knack paddywhack,
   give a dog a bone,
This old man came rolling home.

This old man, he played nine;
He played knick-knack on my spine.
With a knick-knack paddywhack,
   give a dog a bone,
This old man came rolling home.

This old man, he played ten;
He played knick-knack once again.
With a knick-knack paddywhack,
   give a dog a bone,
This old man came rolling home.

Alice the Camel

Alice the camel has five humps.
Alice the camel has five humps.
Alice the camel has five humps.
So go, Alice, go.
Alice the camel has four humps.
Alice the camel has four humps.
Alice the camel has four humps.
So go, Alice, go.
(The song continues until Alice has no humps.)

Now, Alice is a horse!

Ten in a Bed

There were ten in a bed,
And the little one said,
"Roll over, roll over!"
So they all rolled over,
And one fell out.

There were nine in a bed,
And the little one said,
"Roll over, roll over!"
So they all rolled over,
And one fell out.

(The song continues until the last verse.)

There was one in a bed,
And the little one said,
"Good night!"

Ten Silly Elephants
Ten silly elephants standing in a line—
One ran away, and then there were nine.
Nine silly elephants standing at the gate—
One went for hay, and then there were eight.

Eight silly elephants counting to eleven—
One saw a mouse, and then there were seven.
Seven silly elephants picking up sticks—
One built a house, and then there were six.

Six silly elephants looking at a hive—
One chased a bee, and then there were five.
Five silly elephants dancing on the floor—
One bumped his knee, and then there were four.

Four silly elephants sitting in a tree—
One fell out, and then there were three.
Three silly elephants wearing something blue—
One gave a shout, and then there were two.

Two silly elephants sitting in the sun—
One went swimming, and then there was one.
One silly elephant looking for some fun—
Went to join the circus, and then there was none!

Engine, Engine, Number Nine
Engine, engine, number nine
Running on Chicago Line,
Please tell me the correct time.
One o'clock, two o'clock,
Three o'clock, four o'clock,
Five o'clock, six o'clock,
Seven o'clock, eight o'clock. Nine!

Ten Little Fingers
I have ten little fingers and ten little toes,
Two little arms and one little nose,
One little mouth and two little ears,
Two little eyes for smiles and tears,
One little head and two little feet,
One little chin which makes me complete!

One, Two, Buckle My Shoe
One, two, buckle my shoe.
Three, four, shut the door.
Five, six, pick up sticks.
Seven, eight, lay them straight.
Nine, ten, let's do it again!

One for the Money
One for the money,
Two for the show,
Three to get ready,
And four to go!

Three Men in a Tub
Rub a dub dub,
Three men in a tub
And who do you
Think they be?
The butcher, the baker,
The candlestick maker,
Toss them out—all three.

Five Live Fish
One, two, three, four, five,
Catching fishes all alive.
Why did you let them go?
Because they bit my finger so.
Which finger did they bite?
The little finger on the right.

Two Little Blackbirds
Two little blackbirds,   Come back, Jack.
Sitting on the hill.   Come back, Jill.
One named Jack.   Two little blackbirds,
One named Jill.   Sitting on the hill.
Fly away, Jack.   One named Jack.
Fly away, Jill.   One named Jill.

Dominoes

1	one	2
two	3	three
4	four	5

five

6

six

7

seven

8

eight

9

nine

10	ten	11
12	13	14
15	16	17

18	19	20
21	22	23
24	25	26

27 | 28 | 29

30 | + | −

= | < | >

Unit 15: Adjectives–Opposites

Introduction

Using the concept of opposites is one of the best ways to introduce adjectives (words that describe). Children are able to "see" the adjective, which makes understanding the new vocabulary much easier.

Copy the word and photo cards found on pages 168 to176 on card stock. You may use either the word or photo cards, depending upon your students' abilities. Put the cards in the correct opposites pairs and say the words with the class. Next, give each child one opposite card. Have children walk around the room to discover who has their matching opposites. Once children have found each other, have them stand together and read their words for the class.

Pantomiming Opposites Pairs

Have each child find a partner. Give each of the partners a set of opposites cards—for example, one pair of children might be given the opposites cards *young* and *old*. The two children would each pantomime one of the cards while the rest of the class guesses the opposite words. For example, the child who has the *young* card might pantomime crying or crawling like a baby while the child with the *old* card might walk hunched over and pretend he is holding a cane.

The Opposite World

Have children imagine living in an opposite world. For example, things that are little, such as bugs, would now be big, and big things like elephants would now be little. The things that are fast (rabbits running) would now be slow, and things that are slow (turtles crawling) would now be fast. Discuss what it would be like to live in a world where everything was inside out and upside down. Ask children to draw pictures of what they think opposite world might look like!

Opposites Train

Tell children they are going to ride a special train. Choose one child to be the train's engineer. Tell each child a word and ask for the opposite word. For example, say, "black," and the child should say, "white." If the child is correct, she receives a ticket to ride on the train. Continue until all of the children are on the train. When the train is full, have the engineer lead all of the children around the classroom.

Opposites Collage

Provide children with construction paper, scissors, glue, and large sheets of newsprint or manila paper. Instruct them to cut long and short pieces of construction paper to glue on their large sheets of paper.

Other opposites collages: Have students use their imaginations to create other opposites collages such as day/night, black/white, big/little, fast/slow, and young/old.

Cut and Match Opposites Game Cards (Page 167)

Copy page 167 for each student. Have students cut out the 12 pictures. Students should look at the pictures carefully to determine the pairs of opposites. Then, on a separate sheet of paper, have children glue the matching opposites cards side by side.

The following illustrations provide an answer key for the Cut and Match Opposites Game.

The Grand Old Duke of York

The grand old Duke of York,
He had ten thousand men.
He marched them up the hill, and
He marched them down again.

And when you're up, you're up.
And when you're down, you're down.
And when you're only half way up,
You're neither up nor down.

Oh Where, Oh Where Has My Little Dog Gone?

Oh where, oh where has my little *(or substitute the word* big*)* dog gone?
Oh where, oh where can he be?
With his ears cut short and his tail cut long,
Oh where, oh where can he be?

Opposite Song

(sung to the tune of "The Bear Went Over the Mountain")
Front and back are two sides,
Big and little two sizes,
Happy and sad are two moods,
Dirty and clean are disguises!

Off and on goes the switch,
Fast and slow goes the race,
In and out goes our dog all day,
Tied and untied goes my shoelace.

Cut and Match Opposites Game Cards

front

back

young

old

awake

asleep

girl

boy

wet

dry

big

little

cold

hot

happy

sad

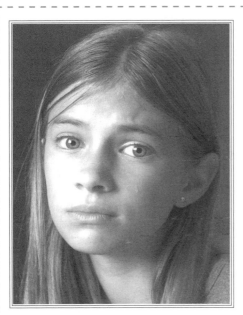

tall

short

full

empty

in

out

clean

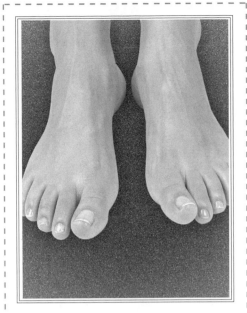

dirty

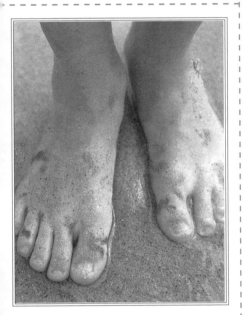

day

night

closed

open

loud

quiet

on

few

many

fast

slow

hard

soft

old

new

Unit 16: Prepositions

Introduction

Introduce prepositions as new vocabulary words rather than as parts of speech. Use a chair to demonstrate these new words for children. Stand next to the chair, sit on it, hold your hand over it, put your hand under it, stand behind it, and so on as you use the new vocabulary.

It is also fun to use blocks to make a small window that can stand alone. Use a small toy bird or one cut from construction paper. The bird can fly over the window, under the window, around the window, through the window, or sit on, next to, or below the window, and so on.

Going on a Bear Hunt

Ask one student to step outside the classroom while the other students decide where to hide a teddy bear or other animal you choose to use. Once the bear has been hidden, the child can come back into the classroom and begin to hunt for the bear.

Encourage the child to ask questions using the positional concepts, for example, "Is the bear on a shelf?" "Is the bear under a chair?" The other students should reply, "Yes, it is," or "No, it isn't." Provide a great deal of practice. Young children also enjoy hunting (and asking questions) in pairs.

Going on a Bear Hunt Chant
(Slap alternate thighs rhythmically.)

Refrain:
We're going on a bear hunt. *(children repeat)*
We're going to catch a bear. *(children repeat)*
A really big bear. *(children repeat)*
We're not afraid! *(children repeat)*

What's that up ahead? *(children repeat)*
It's some tall, tall grass. *(children repeat)*
We can't go over it. *(children repeat)*
We can't go under it. *(children repeat)*
We have to go through it! *(children repeat)*
   (push away grass—say, "swish, swish, swish")
Whoo! That was hard work! *(children repeat)*

Repeat refrain.

What's that up ahead? *(children repeat)*
It's a great big tree *(children repeat)*
We can't go under it. *(children repeat)*
We can't go through it. *(children repeat)*
We have to climb over it! *(children repeat)*
   (climbing motions—say, "woosh, woosh, woosh")
Whoo! That was hard work. *(children repeat)*

Repeat refrain.

What's that up ahead? *(children repeat)*
It's a deep, deep river! *(children repeat)*
We can't go over it. *(children repeat)*
We can't go under it. *(children repeat)*
We'll have to swim through it! *(children repeat)*
   (swimming motions—say, "splash, splash, splash")
Whoo! That was hard work. *(children repeat)*

Repeat refrain.

What's that up ahead? *(children repeat)*
It's a gloomy, dark cave! *(children repeat)*
We can't go over it. *(children repeat)*
We can't go under it. *(children repeat)*
We'll have to go in it. *(children repeat)*
   (tip toeing—say Shhh! Shhh! Shhh!)

Repeat refrain.

Oh no! It's dark in here! *(children repeat)*
I feel something big! *(children repeat)*
It has lots of hair! *(children repeat)*
And very sharp teeth! *(children repeat)*
IT'S A GREAT BIG BEAR! *(children repeat and then scream)*

(Speed up thigh slapping and chanting.)

Quick! Run out of the cave! *(children repeat)*
Swim back through the river! *(children repeat)*
   (swimming motions—say, "splash, splash, splash")
Climb back over the tree! *(children repeat)*
   (climbing motions—say, "woosh, woosh, woosh")
Crawl back through the grass! *(children repeat)*
   (push grass motions—say, "swish, swish, swish")
Run into the house *(children repeat)*
And slam the door. BAM! *(children repeat)*
We're not afraid! *(children repeat)*
Are you? (children repeat)

Obstacle Course

One of the most effective ways to teach positional concepts is through the fun of an obstacle course. Children will love to help you design an interesting path. Use chairs, hula hoops, rubber cones, and tables to set up a course where the children can climb up and down, run over and under, crawl in and out, clamber to the bottom and top, and so on. Encourage the use of lots of new vocabulary as children play.

Preposition Treasure Hunt

Send children on a treasure hunt to practice prepositions of location and yes or no questions. Use a poster adhesive, such as Blu Tack®, that can be rolled into a ball and sticks on anything. First model the activity. Give the adhesive to a child and tell her to put it in a difficult-to-find place (for example, on the underside of a desk, on the wall behind a curtain, etc.). Leave the room and give the child a few moments to hide the adhesive. Then, come back in and ask yes or no questions to find it. (Is it on the desk? Is it near the desk? Is it under the chair?) After you find the adhesive, have a student take the questioner's role. In a large class, students may play in pairs.

The Bear Went Over the Mountain

(sung to the tune of "For He's a Jolly Good Fellow")

Sing this song and, as you repeat the lines, change the preposition, for example, up the mountain, around the mountain, through the mountain, next to the mountain, and so on.

The bear went over the mountain,
The bear went over the mountain,
The bear went over the mountain,
To see what he could see.

To see what he could see,
To see what he could see,
But, the other side of the mountain,

The other side of the mountain,
The other side of the mountain,
Was all that he could see.

Was all that he could see,
Was all that he could see,
The other side of the mountain,
Was all that he could see!

Eensy Weensy Spider

The eensy weensy spider
Crawled up the waterspout.
   (fingers climb up other arm)
Down came the rain
   (wiggle fingers down
   from head to waist)
And washed the spider out.
   (throw arms to sides)
Out came the sun and
dried up all the rain,
   (raise hands above head;
   make circle for sun)
And the eensy weensy spider
Crawled up the spout again.
   (fingers climb up arm again)

Variation: Vary other position words in the rhyme, such as crawled *over*, crawled *around*, crawled *next to*, crawled *under*, and so on. Use a spider cutout and draw a spout to act out the rhyme.

Polly Put the Kettle On

Polly put the kettle on,
Polly put the kettle on,
Polly put the kettle on,
We'll all have tea.

Suki take it off again,
Suki take it off again,
Suki take it off again,
We'll all have none.

Polly put it back again,
Polly put it back again,
Polly put it back again,
We'll all have tea.

Busy Day

(sung to the tune of "Baa, Baa, Black Sheep")

In the house, and
Running out the door,
On the swing, then
To the store!
Through the gate and
Right between the yards,
Then inside to
Play some cards.
Over the fence and
Underneath the tree,
These are places
You'll find me!

Name _____

Prepositions–Read and Draw a . . .

 rabbit <u>under</u> the table	 fish <u>in</u> the bowl	 child <u>in</u> the middle
 bird <u>over</u> the tree	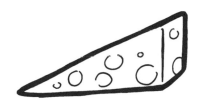 mouse <u>on</u> the cheese	 ant <u>under</u> the ground
 dog <u>next to</u> the house	 cat <u>in</u> the basket	 cloud <u>over</u> the house

 boy rabbit ant mouse cloud fish cat dog bird

Let's Play "I Spy!"

This is a wonderful game for teaching prepositions. Look around the room and choose a toy or some object that the children are familiar with. Give clues to help children figure out what object you are thinking about. For example, start the game by saying, "I spy something near the bookshelves." Children then begin asking questions to help them guess the object's identity. (Use plenty of prepositions and position words such as *near*, *by*, *next to*, *over*, *under*, *up*, and *down*.)

around

behind

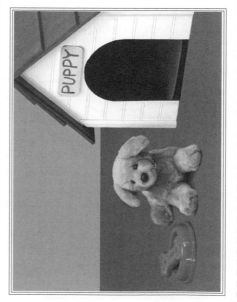

between

beside

far from

in

in front of

next to

on

over

through

under

Unit 17: School

Introduction—People Who Work at School

The names of school tools, the people who work at school, and the places within the school are some of the most important vocabulary words that students need to know.

Take pictures of the adults whom your students have contact with, such as teachers, the nurse, the librarian, the principal, cooks, maintenance staff, and teacher assistants, and make two copies of each photo. Arrange their pictures on a poster and label it with their names. Invite everyone pictured to come into your classroom to meet the children.

Next, draw a simple map of the school. Place the school personnel's other photos in their correct locations, such as the cook in the kitchen. As children become more familiar with their school surroundings and people in the school, allow them to go in pairs to deliver messages.

Label, Label, Label

Copy onto card stock the word and photo cards found on pages 186 to 191. Use these cards as labels for your classroom. At first, use both the word and photos as labels. As children become more familiar with the objects, remove (or cover) the photos so that only the words remain. Eventually, children will begin to associate the printed words with their meanings. This is an effective teaching method for any group of young children or children, of any age, who are being introduced to a new language and want to learn new vocabulary quickly.

Pass the School Tools

Have students sit in a circle and pass a few objects or photo cards of objects from hand to hand under the table or behind their backs without looking at them. Being secretive makes the game more fun. Say, "Stop," and ask, "Who has the pencil?" The students should point to the student that they think has the pencil and say, "_(student's name)_ has the pencil." Give a round of applause to the first student to guess correctly.

Surprise Box

Place a variety of classroom school tools in a box (_pencils, crayons, markers, tape, paper clips, glue, ruler, paper, chalk,_ and _scissors_). One at a time, have the children close their eyes, put a hand into the box, and pull out an object. With practice, children should be able to identify the object simply by touching it.

Learn about School Tools by Experimenting with Them!

Homemade Rainbow Crayons

Fill each section of a muffin tin with broken crayons. To make rainbow crayons, place four or five different colors of crayon pieces in each section. Place in a 400° oven just long enough for the crayons to melt. Watch them carefully, as crayons melt very quickly and the colors will blend together. You want the crayons to become soft—not liquid. Take the pan out of the oven and place it on a cooling rack. After cooling, pop out the crayons and enjoy coloring!

Soapy Flakes Paint

Use an electric mixer to beat soap flakes and water together until creamy. While freshly whipped, have students finger paint on dark-colored pieces of paper. You can also add powered tempera paint to color the mixture and keep on painting.

Smelly Glue

Pour a small amount of white glue into several paper cups. Add some Kool-Aid® or other drink mix powder. This activity is even more fun if you have several different flavors available. Have children paint the "flavored" glue onto paper or a paper plate. Make the drink from some of the drink mix so that children can also taste what they are seeing and smelling. Let them touch the glue when it is dry and have them smell their fingers. Did the scent rub off onto their fingertips?

Puffy Paint

Mix equal parts of flour, salt, and water together in a bowl. Add tempera paint for color. Mix well and pour into a squeeze bottle that has a narrow nozzle. Students can squeeze the puffy paint onto cardboard or a heavy stock paper. The paint mixture will become hard as it dries.

Colorful Tissue Paper

Have students tear colorful tissue paper into small shapes and set them aside. Mix two parts glue and one part water in a paper cup. Students can paint this diluted glue on white construction paper and place the tissue paper shapes, one at a time, all over the wet glue. The variety of colors and shapes of the tissue paper will make for some interesting designs. When the paper is dry, students can brush the diluted glue over the tissue paper again to create a smooth, varnish-like finish.

Snipping Funny Shapes

Let children enjoy cutting pieces from colored construction paper. It does not matter how big or what shapes the pieces are. Cut and remove the backing from 8.5" x 11" (22 cm x 28 cm) pieces of clear contact paper. When each child has a small pile of colored shapes, she can simply stick the shapes to the contact paper. When finished, the contact paper can be turned over and applied to another sheet of paper. The result is a work of scissor art ready for display.

Scissor Cutting Magazines and Catalogs

This activity is very educational and is also an activity children will enjoy doing for long periods of time. Simply provide children with magazines or catalogs and let them cut out pictures and use glue sticks to glue the pictures onto paper. This activity can also help children learn how to categorize and sort. Have children cut out pictures and sort them into specified categories, such as people, furniture, clothes, or food.

School Tools Reproducible Activity

Copy page 185 for each student. Have children draw their favorite school tools on the pictured tabletop. This can also be used as a receptive language activity. Say the name of a school tool and children should draw that tool on the tabletop.

School Day

(sung to the tune of "Blow the Man Down")

The chalk on the chalkboard helps us to write,
The clock can tell us the time,
Crayons and paints make our pictures so bright,
And one lunchbox holds the lunch that is mine!

We can look at a globe to see the whole world,
Then we all play a great game,
On the playground, we run and rocket and twirl,
At the library, getting books is our aim!

With glue and with paste we can make paper stick,
With scissors, we cut out cool shapes,
A stapler holds pages together so quick,
And we can add pictures by using some tape!

I love to use blocks to build a tall tower,
An easel holds pictures so well,
At school, all this learning gives me the power
To make things, to say things, to read and to spell!

Name _____

School Tools

(Directions found on page 184.)

blocks		**books**
	**chalk**	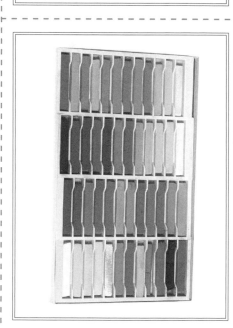
chalkboard		**classroom**

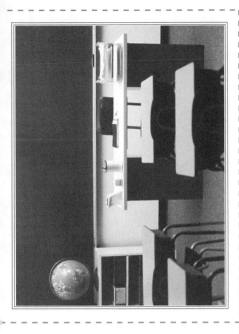

clock

computer

crayons

desk

easel

game

globe

glue
&
paste

library

lunch box

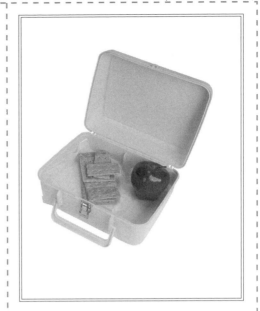

notebook

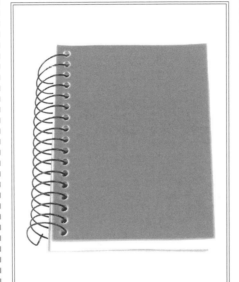

paint

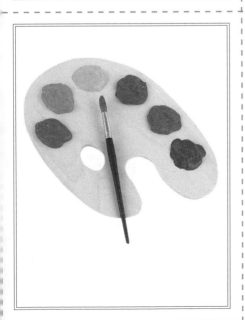

paper

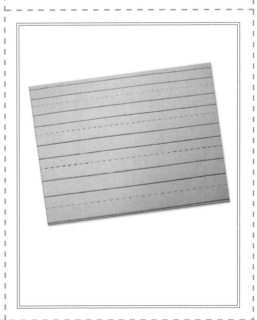

pen

pencil

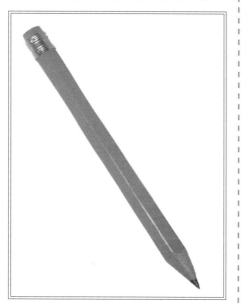

pencil sharpener

playground

ruler

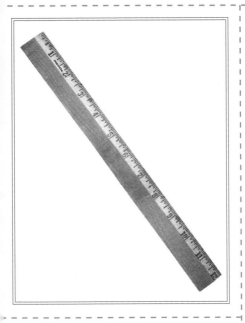

school

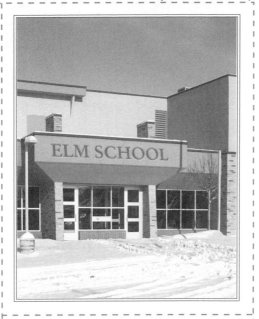

scissors

stapler

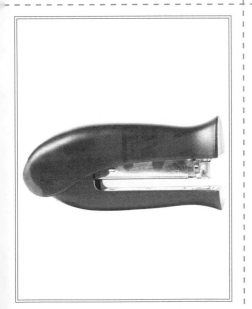

wastebasket

Unit 18: Sports and Leisure Activities

Introduction

Having a hobby or playing a sport may not be part of the culture of some of your students. Even common toys and leisure time activities may be different from what your students understand or have experienced. This unit will provide some opportunities for young children to learn about some American sports, toys, and leisure activities.

What Sports Do You Like?

Have children brainstorm a list of sports. Place a photo or draw a picture next to each word that represents that sport. How many children have played the sport? Graph children's participation in the sports. Which is the most popular? Then, teach students some new outside games such as four square, basketball, softball, volleyball, badminton, roller skating, etc.

My Hobby

You can adapt the content here to the age and ability level of the children in your class. This is an opportunity for children to talk about something they like or enjoy doing.

❖ Make a list of all of the children's special interests. Each child can draw a picture of his favorite hobby or interest and write key words or a short sentence associated with it.

❖ Ask children to bring something from home representing their hobbies or interests that they can share with the rest of the class. Some of these interests may be specific to the children's cultures. Some children may even collect items that are from their native countries. This is a great way to learn about each student's culture.

Music

This activity could involve playing instruments, learning about instruments that are popular in certain countries, or learning that some children may actually be taking music lessons from a parent, family member, or another adult. Listening to music always seems to be a favorite activity of children. Music can also be an effective tool in an English classroom for developing an awareness of rhythm in language.

❖ Ask children to bring CDs of their favorite music to class.

❖ Play music and have students close their eyes and tap their fingers or feet to the beat.

❖ Talk about adjectives such as *fast*, *slow*, *quiet*, and *loud*. Listen to music and then ask children to describe it. Encourage them to use the new vocabulary words.

❖ Ask children to close their eyes and listen carefully to a piece of music. Then, have them draw a picture of something the music made them think about. Have them share their drawings and describe what they drew.

Musical Instruments

Let children make musical instruments that they can play while you are enjoying music in the classroom. Here are some easy instruments that the children can make:

Spoon Timekeepers: Show students how to tap the bowls of two metal spoons together in time to music. Try tapping the handles together for a different sound. Children may tie two spoons together with a bit of yarn at the base of the bowls to make a castanet.

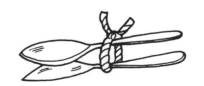

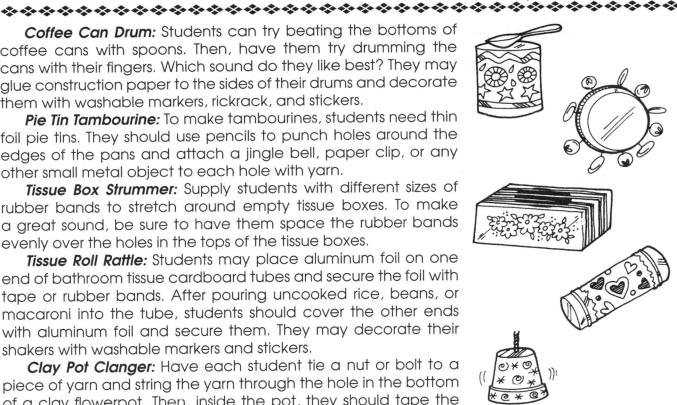

Coffee Can Drum: Students can try beating the bottoms of coffee cans with spoons. Then, have them try drumming the cans with their fingers. Which sound do they like best? They may glue construction paper to the sides of their drums and decorate them with washable markers, rickrack, and stickers.

Pie Tin Tambourine: To make tambourines, students need thin foil pie tins. They should use pencils to punch holes around the edges of the pans and attach a jingle bell, paper clip, or any other small metal object to each hole with yarn.

Tissue Box Strummer: Supply students with different sizes of rubber bands to stretch around empty tissue boxes. To make a great sound, be sure to have them space the rubber bands evenly over the holes in the tops of the tissue boxes.

Tissue Roll Rattle: Students may place aluminum foil on one end of bathroom tissue cardboard tubes and secure the foil with tape or rubber bands. After pouring uncooked rice, beans, or macaroni into the tube, students should cover the other ends with aluminum foil and secure them. They may decorate their shakers with washable markers and stickers.

Clay Pot Clanger: Have each student tie a nut or bolt to a piece of yarn and string the yarn through the hole in the bottom of a clay flowerpot. Then, inside the pot, they should tape the yarn to the top of the pot to make a clapper. Finally, they can decorate the clangers with washable markers.

Be a Good Sport! (Page 194)

This is a wonderful unit for teaching the importance of good sportsmanship. A child who learns to be a good sport and who understands a game's rules will have an easier time socially. Use the reproducible Good Sport Award on page 194 as an incentive for children. Here are some good rules to teach:

1. Don't cheat!
2. Be a polite winner, not a sore loser.
3. Be fair and kind when choosing teams.
4. Don't throw objects into the air or onto the field.
5. Encourage your teammates.
6. Don't block another person's view.
7. Don't argue with the referee/official.
8. Take turns and share.

Take Me Out to the Ball Game

Take me out to the ball game,
Take me out with the crowd.
Buy me some peanuts and Cracker Jack,
I don't care if I never get back.
Let me root, root, root for the home team,
If they don't win, it's a shame.
For it's one, two, three strikes, you're out,
At the old ball game.

Our Favorite Hobbies
(sung to the tune of "Frère Jacques")
Jen plays baseball,
Chen plays football,
Taylor bikes,
Maria hikes!
Jamal rides his skateboard,
Jill can play guitar chords,
I like planes in flight,
And to run with all my might!

Ann likes sledding,
Bill likes swimming,
Jay likes cars,
Cho loves stars!
Keisha loves her singing,
I send kites a-winging,
Very far! Very far!

Be a Good Sport!

GOOD SPORT AWARD

Presented to:

_____

because _____

_____

signed by _____

TEAM WORK

ball

baseball

basketball

bike

car

dancing

doll

fishing

football

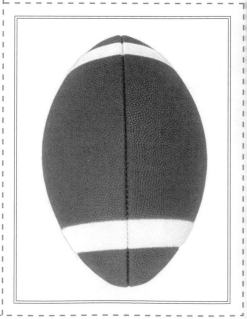

hopscotch

kite

marbles

painting

pets

piano

roller blades

running

singing

skateboard

soccer

tennis

video games

Unit 19: Transportation

Introduction
Introduce this unit by leading students in a discussion about how they all get to school. Do they ride a bus, walk with a parent or friend, ride a bike, or ride in a car or van? Make a chart of all of the students' responses. Which is the most common form of transportation to school? Which is the least common?

Land-Water-Air Bulletin Board
This bulletin board is a wonderful way to show children many different types of transportation. Design the background of this bulletin board so that part of the bulletin board is sky, part has roads and land, and part is a body of water. You may also choose to involve children in the creation of the background. When the background is complete, children can either cut out pictures of transportation vehicles or they can create their own by drawing and coloring many different means of transportation for the three categories:

Land	Water	Air
car	raft	balloon
truck	canoe	blimp
train	sailing ship	glider
motorcycle	steamship	airplane
bus	barge	jet
bicycle	freighter	helicopter
van	speedboat	rocket
ambulance	tugboat	
rollerblades	submarine	
walking		

Traffic Light Project and Game
Using three small paper plates, have each child create a traffic light. The first plate should be painted red, the second plate yellow, and the third plate green.

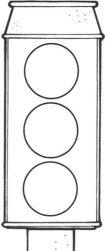

❖ Teach students the following rhyme:
Red on top means stop, stop, stop! Green below means go, go, go!
Also, explain that when children see a yellow light, they should slow down and then stop.

❖ Let children play with their traffic lights. Choose one person to be the traffic light controller. Tell the children to pretend to be driving cars. Have the controller hold up the traffic light and cover two of the colors. The rest of the children should obey the color that is being displayed.

Go World, Go!
(sung to the tune of "Humpty Dumpty")

Fire trucks go roaring past,
The school bus takes us off to school,
Planes fly high and
Sailboats glide,
And motorcycles are so cool!

Ambulances rush to help,
Bicycles whir in the park,
Trucks rumble along,
Jeeps are so strong,
And cars have lights for when it is dark!

The Bus Song

(Roll hands over each other.)
The wheels on the bus go round and round,
Round and round, round and round.
The wheels on the bus go round and round
All through the town.

(Put arms together in front of you and "swish" like windshield wipers.)
The wipers on the bus go "Swish, swish, swish,
Swish, swish, swish, swish, swish, swish."
The wipers on the bus go "Swish, swish, swish,"
All through the town.

(Cover eyes with hands on "shut" and uncover them on "open.")
The door on the bus goes open and shut,
Open and shut, open and shut.
The door on the bus goes open and shut
All through the town.

(Pretend to honk horn.)
The horn on the bus goes "Beep, beep, beep,
Beep, beep, beep, beep, beep, beep."
The horn on the bus goes "Beep, beep, beep,"
All through the town.

(Pretend to fill tank using pointer finger as gas nozzle)
The gas on the bus goes "Glunk, glunk, glunk,
Glunk, glunk, glunk, glunk, glunk, glunk."
The gas on the bus goes "Glunk, glunk, glunk,"
All through the town.

(Pretend to put money in the cash box on the bus.)
The money on the bus goes "Clink, clink, clink,
Clink, clink, clink, clink, clink, clink."
The money on the bus goes "Clink, clink, clink,"
All through the town.

(Put fisted hands in front of eyes and rub them like a baby crying)
The baby on the bus says, "Wah, wah, wah!
Wah, wah, wah, wah, wah, wah!"
The baby on the bus says, "Wah, wah, wah!"
All through the town.

(Put pointer finger to mouth to "shhh.")
The people on the bus say, "Shh, shh, shh,
Shh, shh, shh, shh, shh, shh."
The people on the bus say, "Shh, shh, shh,"
All through the town.

(Point to self on "I," right hand over heart on "love," and point to another on "you.")
The mommy on the bus says, "I love you,
I love you, I love you."
The daddy on the bus says, "I love you, too,"
All through the town.

Traffic Signs and Safety

Name _____

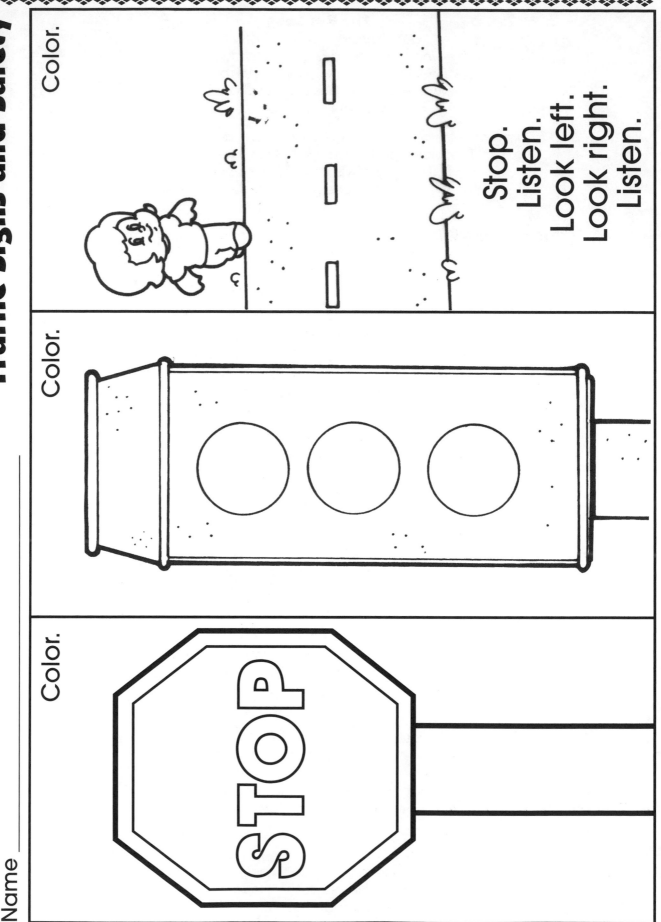

Color.

Stop.
Listen.
Look left.
Look right.
Listen.

Color.

Color.

STOP

airplane

ambulance

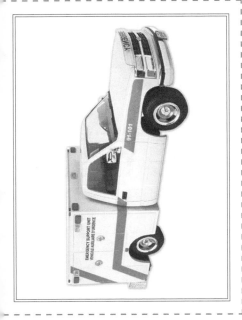

bicycle

bulldozer

canoe

car

city bus

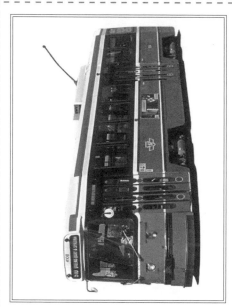

fire truck

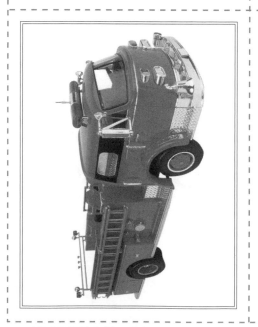

helicopter

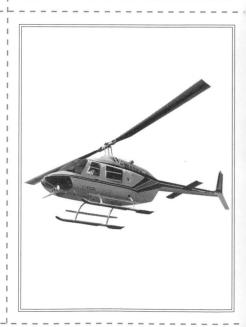

hot air balloon

jeep

motorcycle

police car

sailboat

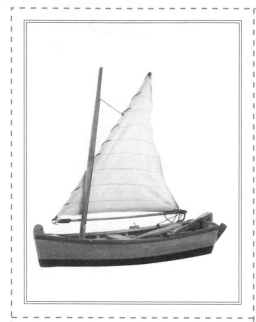

school bus

skateboard

speedboat

train

truck

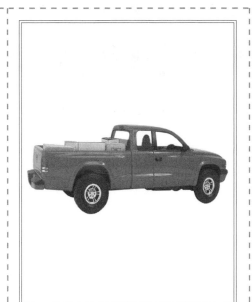

van

wagon

wheelchair

Unit 20: Verbs–Actions

Introduction–Following Classroom Directions (Page 210)

Being able to understand and follow simple classroom directions is an essential skill that young children need to function well in the classroom. The use of gestures can often help relay the meaning of your directions. Make a copy of the chart on page 210 for each child. Demonstrate each of the gestures as you say the words. Then, let children practice the words and actions with one another.

Variation: Choose one child to be the zookeeper, and the other children will be monkeys. Have the zookeeper demonstrate one of the gestures on the Following Classroom Directions chart as the monkeys mimic the zookeeper's action. If a child performs a wrong movement that child must sit down. The last child standing is the winner and will become the next zookeeper. Increase the challenge of the game by having the zookeeper perform two actions in row.

Follow the Leader

Play the traditional game of follow the leader. Have students line up behind you and follow the actions you perform. As you play, name each action and have children repeat each word after you. Repeat several times, using the same actions and corresponding words. Then, give students a chance to be the leader.

When children have become familiar with the new action vocabulary words, have them line up and begin to walk around the room. Say an action word without demonstrating the word's meaning and see if children can follow the direction simply by hearing the oral command.

Action Race

This is a fun game using a variety of actions such as walking, jumping, hopping, clapping, running, crawling, skipping, galloping, and so on. Divide students into two teams. Have children sit in lines with one chair beside each team and one chair at the other end of the room from each team. The first student from each team stands next to the team's chair. Call out an action such as "walk." The first two students must then walk to the chairs on the other side of the room, walk back, sit down in their team's chairs, and say, "I can walk." The first player to follow the directions correctly and complete her turn wins a point for her team. Continue the game with a new action.

Stand, Walk, and Sit Musical Chairs

Place chairs back-to-back in two lines. The number of chairs should be one fewer than the number of children playing. Instead of listening to music, children will listen to and follow your oral instructions to stand, walk, or sit. When you say "walk," the children should walk around the chairs. As soon as you say "sit," children should find a chair and sit as quickly as possible. The child without a chair will be the next person to say the instructions. Have that child tell the children to stand. Then, remove another chair and begin the game again.

Obstacle Course

Set up an obstacle course using cones, boxes, mats, hula hoops, or whatever else you may have available. Tell children they will go through the obstacle course one at a time. As the first child moves through the course, call out an action vocabulary word. Then, children may take turns calling out an action for each child on the course to perform.

Jumping, Rolling, Running, or Walking Races

The children should each find a partner. One child in each pair (partner A) should stand at one end of the room and each of the other partners (partner B) should stand at the other end of the room. Call out a vocabulary action word such as *jump, roll, run,* or *walk.* Partner A's must perform the action to reach their partner B's on the other side of the room. Once each partner A is close to his partner, the partners should tag each other by clapping hands. Then, call out another action word. Partner B's must perform the new action to get back to the other side of the room.

Verb Dance

(sung to the tune of "Hokey Pokey")

I brush my hair and teeth,
I wash my hands just right.
I eat my breakfast, and
My mom hugs me tight.
Then to school I run,
We learn and have some fun,
And that makes my day so bright!

I go to class to dance,
Then back home I go.
I help to rake some leaves,
And I get a ball to throw.
At dinnertime,
We laugh and talk and dine,
And then off to bed I go!

Skip to My Lou

Skip, skip, skip to my Lou,
Skip, skip, skip to my Lou,
Skip, skip, skip to my Lou,
Skip to my Lou, my darlin'.

Fly's in the buttermilk. Shoo, fly, shoo,
Fly's in the buttermilk. Shoo, fly, shoo,
Fly's in the buttermilk. Shoo, fly, shoo,
Skip to my Lou, my darlin'.

To give children more TPR experiences, sing this song again and change the verb, for example, children can jump to my Lou, hop to my Lou, crawl to my Lou, and so on.

The Ants Go Marching One by One

The ants go marching one by one, hurrah, hurrah.
The ants go marching one by one, hurrah, hurrah.
The ants go marching one by one,
The little one stops to suck his thumb,
And they all go marching down into the ground
To get out of the rain, BOOM! BOOM! BOOM!

The ants go marching two by two . . .
The little one stops to tie her shoe . . .

The ants go marching three by three . . .
The little one stops to climb a tree . . .

The ants go marching four by four . . .
The little one stops to shut the door . . .

The ants go marching five by five . . .
The little one stops to take a dive . . .

The ants go marching six by six . . .
The little one stops to pick up sticks . . .

The ants go marching seven by seven . . .
The little one stops to go to heaven . . .

The ants go marching eight by eight . . .
The little one stops to jump the gate . . .

The ants go marching nine by nine . . .
The little one stops to scratch his spine . . .

The ants go marching ten by ten . . .
The little one stops to say, "The end!"

Following Classroom Directions

line up	raise your hand	open your book

close your book	**work with a friend**	**look**

listen	**clean up**	**write your name**

pay attention	**cut**	**come here**

bathe

brush
hair

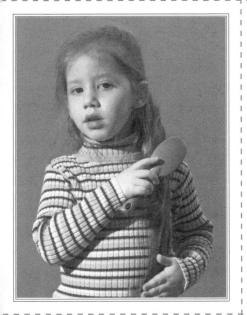

build

camp

climb

color

cook

crawl

cry

cut

dance

drink

eat

fight

float

hug

jump

kiss

laugh

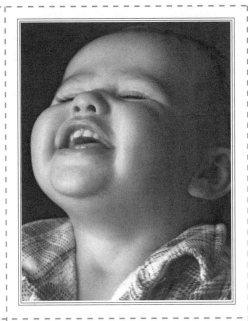

listen

look

paint

peek

play

pull

push

rake

read

ride

run

sing

sit

skate

skip

sleep

slide

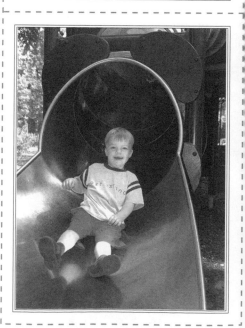

smell

smile

sneeze

splash

stand

swim

swing

talk

think

throw

tickle

wait

walk

wash

wave

work

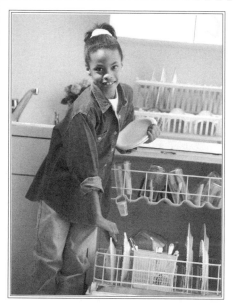

write

zip

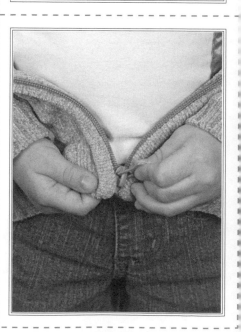

Unit 21: Weather

Introduction

Weather is a topic that is discussed daily in nearly every classroom. Children need to learn words that describe weather conditions as well as the words that will help them dress properly for those weather conditions.

Weather Wheel

Cut a large circle out of tagboard. Divide the circle into four sections. In each section, draw and color a picture depicting a certain weather condition. Attach an arrow to the center of the circle using a brass fastener.

Each day, choose a child to act as the weatherperson. The daily weatherperson should move the arrow to the picture showing that day's weather conditions. Encourage the weatherperson to use descriptive vocabulary and give recommendations about the clothing everyone should wear when playing outside. You may provide additional props such as a large map and a microphone for the weatherperson's report.

Weather Windows and Weather Warren

Draw and color the figure of a child on a large piece of tagboard and cut it out. Place pieces of the hook side of self-stick Velcro® on the top of the figure's head and on its shoulders, hands, waist, and feet. Make tagboard clothing for various weather conditions and attach the loop side of the Velcro® pieces to the clothing. Introduce the character to your students as Weather Warren.

Draw four windows on pieces of tagboard. On one side of each window, simply draw windowpanes. On the other side, draw various weather conditions. Attach a string to each window so that it can be hung on the bulletin board, displaying either side. Each morning, invite two children to serve as weather people. One child may dress Warren correctly for the weather, and the other child may change the weather window to reflect the current weather outside.

Let's Make Rain

Heat water in a teakettle. Hold a glass jar over the spout of the kettle to collect steam. Compare the steam to fog or rain clouds. The air outside the jar is colder, so droplets will form inside the jar and fall down like real raindrops.

Use this science activity as an opportunity to practice new vocabulary. Ask students to describe what they see. Discuss the experiment using the related word and photo cards on pages 226 to 228, such as *cloudy*, *foggy*, and *raining*.

Wind and Air

When exploring the concepts of wind and air with English language learners, it is helpful to use a visual example. Sailboat experiments are a good way to show students what the words *wind* and *air* mean.

Construct simple sailboats (see illustration). Float the sailboats in a container of water. Talk about the fact that when the air is not moving, there is no wind, and the boats are still. Have children take turns playing the part of the wind by blowing through straws to move the boats across the water. Encourage the use of weather vocabulary as students play.

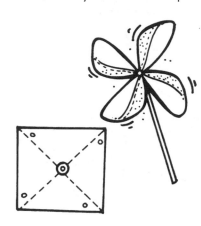

Pinwheel

Students can make pinwheels for another opportunity to practice weather vocabulary. Cut paper into 6" x 6" (15 cm x 15 cm) squares. Have students draw two diagonal lines on their squares that connect opposite corners and then trace a penny in the center. Next, students should make four cuts on the diagonal lines to the edge of the circle in the center. Help them punch holes in their pinwheels as shown at left. Each student should punch a hole through the top of a straw and then fold, without creasing, each corner to the center, attaching the four corners and straw together with a brass fastener. Have students take their pinwheels outside and watch them spin!

Rain, Rain, Go Away

Rain, rain, go away.
Come again another day.
All the children want to play.

Oh, Susanna!

I come from Alabama
With my banjo on my knee.
I'm going to Louisiana,
My true love for to see.
It rained all night the day I left,
The weather it was dry.
The sun so hot, I froze to death.
Susanna, don't you cry

Oh, Susanna!
Oh don't you cry for me
For I come from Alabama
With my banjo on my knee.

All the Seasons

*(sung to the tune of
"London Bridge")*
When it's sunny, it is bright,
Clouds make it as dark as night,
When it snows the world is white,
I love seasons!

You Are My Sunshine

You are my sunshine,
My only sunshine.
You make me happy
When skies are gray,
You'll never know, dear,
How much I love you.
Please don't take my sunshine away

The other night, dear, as I lay sleeping,
I dreamed I held you in my arms.
When I awoke, dear, I was mistaken,
And I hung my head and cried.

You are my sunshine,
My only sunshine.
You make me happy
When skies are gray.
You'll never know, dear,
How much I love you.
Please don't take my sunshine away.

On windy days, the trees all dance,
Fog puts the air in a trance,
Rain gives growing things a chance,
I love seasons!

Name _____

Match the Person to the Weather

Directions: Have students color the pictures of the children and cut them out along the dotted lines. Students should glue each picture in the correct season and finish coloring the page.

autumn

cloudy

foggy

lightning

moon
&
stars

raining

rainbow

snowing

spring

summer

sunny

windy

winter

Unit 22: Wild Animals

Introduction

Children love learning about animals, especially the animals that are considered wild. The study of animals can encourage all sorts of new vocabulary and conversations.

Zoo Game

Animal noises is a fun activity for children. Copy the word and photo cards found on pages 232 to 237 on card stock. Show the photos and introduce the name of each animal and the noise or sound made by the animal. Hand each student a photo card without showing the other students what is on the card. Have children make the noises of their animals while the other children guess which animals are being imitated.

Design Your Own Zoo

Tell the children that they will design and build their own zoo. Ask each of them to bring in a stuffed animal and any extra boxes they might have at home, such as shoe boxes, cereal boxes, etc.

Talk about the type of environment or habitat that would be best for each animal. Does the animal need trees? Water? Rocks to climb on? Design and make things that would be best for each animal's environment. Simply making each model habitat will stimulate all sorts of new and descriptive vocabulary.

Continue the study of animals by learning about what kinds of food each animal needs to stay healthy. How much exercise does it need? What climate is best? The possibilities for enriching vocabulary are endless.

Nonfiction Information

Use the following factual information to create a classroom big book. Print the information on each page and let children create illustrations to go with each animal.

Lion: The lion is called the "King of the Beasts" because lions are so strong and fierce. A lion can grow up to 11 feet long and weigh 500 pounds. Lions sleep during the day and hunt at night. Only male lions have manes, which start to grow when they are about two years old.

Elephant: The elephant is the world's largest land animal. Elephants can be 11 feet tall and weigh up to 14,000 pounds. They use their huge ears as fans. An elephant will spend 16 hours a day eating!

Zebra: The zebra looks like a striped horse. Zebras might look like horses, but they are stubborn and not as gentle as horses. You cannot ride a zebra. Their stripes help them hide in the tall grasses.

Giraffe: The giraffe is the tallest animal in the world. It can be 18 feet tall and weigh 4,000 pounds. A giraffe's neck can be six feet long. Giraffes can see in all directions without moving their heads. They like to eat leaves and shoots and sometimes seeds, pods, and fruit.

Ostrich: The ostrich is the world's largest bird. They can be eight feet tall and weigh between 200 and 300 pounds. Ostriches have great eyesight and can see for several miles. An ostrich will eat anything!

Hippopotamus: The hippo is the second largest land animal. Although their name means "river horse," and they resemble pigs, hippos are closely related to whales. The hippo can grow to 12 feet long and weigh 8,000 pounds. Hippos love the water. Most hippo babies can swim before they can walk on land.

Rhinoceros: The rhinoceros is another huge animal. It can weigh up to 4,000 pounds and grow as long as 12 feet. The rhino is actually a relative of the horse. It can even run as fast as a horse. The rhino is easily identified by its horns, which are made from claw and hairlike materials.

Safari Bulletin Board

Copy the photo pattern below. Have children draw their favorite wild animals. Display the pictures on a bulletin board with the caption, "Photo Safari."

Animal Friends

(sung to the tune of "You Are My Sunshine")
An alligator has big white teeth, dear,
An elephant is huge and gray,
The owl asks you who you are, dear,
And the monkey just wants to play.

The dolphin glides through
        the deep blue sea, dear,
A snake may scare you in the grass,
A squirrel can leap from tree to tree, dear,
And the quick fox, dear, will never be last.

The bear will sleep all winter long, dear,
A tiger hunts in the jungle wild,
The seal can slip through the icy waves, dear,
And the wolf has a pup as its child.

The world is filled with so many creatures,
And they all share our earth today.
They are each one so very fine, dear,
We must make sure these friends always stay!

Going to the Zoo

Daddy's taking me to the zoo tomorrow, zoo tomorrow, zoo tomorrow.
Daddy's taking me to the zoo tomorrow, and we're going to stay all day.
We're going to the zoo, zoo, zoo,
How about you, you, you?
You can come too, too, too,
We're going to the zoo, zoo, zoo.

Name _____

Hidden Wild Animals

Directions: Have students circle the hidden animals, the equipment needed for a jungle safari, and the monkey's lunch. Children should compare and discuss what they found. Then, they may color the page.

alligator

bear

bee

dolphin

elephant

flamingo

fox

frog

giraffe

gorilla

hippopotamus

ladybug

leopard

lion

monkey

owl

ostrich

penguin

rhinoceros

seal

shark

snake

squirrel

tiger

whale

wolf

zebra

Standards Correlations

English Language Learners: Building Vocabulary Games & Activities

This book supports the NCTE/IRA Standards for the English Language Arts and the recommended teaching practices outlined in the NAEYC/IRA position statement Learning to Read and Write: Developmentally Appropriate Practices for Young Children.

NCTE/IRA Standards for the English Language Arts

Each activity in this book supports one or more of the following standards:

1. **Students read many different types of print and nonprint texts for a variety of purposes.** Many of the games and activities in this book require students to read both words and pictures. In addition, there are suggestions in the book for activities such as readers' theater, choral reading, and literature suggestions in which students read different types of texts.

2. **Students read literature from various time periods, cultures, and genres in order to form an understanding of humanity.** The literature chapter in *Vocabulary Building Games & Activities* has a literature list that can be used for read-alouds and for student reading. This list includes literature from a wide range of time periods, cultures, and genres.

3. **Students use a variety of strategies to build meaning while reading.** The activities and games in *Vocabulary Building Games & Activities* help students learn a variety of reading skills and strategies, including vocabulary development, making predictions, drawing conclusions, classification, receptive language skills, and sequencing, among others.

4. **Students communicate in spoken, written, and visual form, for a variety of purposes and a variety of audiences.** Students communicate in all three of these forms while doing the activities in *Vocabulary Building Games & Activities*. They communicate in spoken form while playing games, participating in class discussions, and singing songs, in written form by participating in group writing projects and writing letters, words and sentences in selected activities, and in visual form when doing drawings or other art projects as part of selected activities.

5. **Students begin to understand and respect the diversity of language across cultures, regions, ethnicities, and social roles.** Many activities in *Vocabulary Building Games & Activities* have students share information about themselves and their cultures, enabling students to learn about other cultures.

6. **Students whose first language is not English use their first language to learn English and to understand content in all curriculum areas.** *Vocabulary Building Games & Activities* was specifically created for use in English Language Development programs, enabling ELL students to use their knowledge of their first language to learn vocabulary in English.

7. **Students become participating members of a variety of literacy communities.** The group games, songs, and discussions in *Vocabulary Building Games & Activities* are very effective ways for a teacher to begin to build a diverse classroom literacy community.

8. **Students use spoken, written, and visual language for their own purposes, such as to learn for enjoyment, or to share information.** *Vocabulary Building Games & Activities* enables students of many different reading and communication abilities to communicate with others through many different means and for many different reasons.

NAEYC/IRA Position Statement Learning to Read and Write: Developmentally Appropriate Practices for Young Children

Each activity in this book supports one or more of the following recommended teaching practices for Preschool students:

1. **Adults create positive relationships with children by talking with them, modeling reading and writing, and building children's interest in reading and writing.** The many engaging activities in *Vocabulary Building Games & Activities* include extensive conversations and discussions among teachers and students and are very effective in building students' interests in reading and writing.

2. **Teachers provide and draw children's attention to print-rich learning environments.** This book includes many bulletin board and big books for teachers and students to create together, contributing to a print-rich learning environment.

3. **Teachers read to children daily, both as individuals and in small groups. They select high-quality, culturally diverse reading materials.** *Vocabulary Building Games & Activities* includes read-aloud literature suggestions for each thematic unit in the book, along with many activities that incorporate teacher read-alouds.

4. **Teachers provide opportunities for children to discuss what has been read to them, focusing on both language structure and content.** The "Literature" chapter in *Vocabulary Building Games & Activities* includes many suggestions for discussions based on literature.

5. **Teachers provide opportunities for children to participate in literacy play, incorporating both reading and writing.** Most of the thematic units in *Vocabulary Building Games & Activities* have suggestions for learning centers and games that incorporate literacy play.

6. **Teachers provide experiences and materials that help children expand their vocabularies.** Vocabulary building is the main focus of this book, and its games, activities, and photo-word cards provide many ways to accomplish this.

Each activity in this book supports one or more of the following recommended teaching practices for Kindergarten and Primary students:

1. **Teachers read to children daily and provide opportunities for students to independently read both fiction and nonfiction texts.** *Vocabulary Building Games & Activities* includes read-aloud literature suggestions for each thematic unit in the book, along with many activities that incorporate teacher read-alouds.

2. **Teachers provide opportunities for students to write many different kinds of texts for different purposes.** While doing the activities in *Vocabulary Building Games & Activities,* students participate in group writing exercises and have the opportunity to write letters, words, and sentences in the context of games.

3. **Teachers provide opportunities for children to work in small groups.** *Vocabulary Building Games & Activities* includes many small group activities.

4. **Teachers provide challenging instruction that expands children's knowledge of their world and expands vocabulary.** Vocabulary building is the main focus of this book, and its games, activities, and photo-word cards provide many ways to accomplish this. In addition, the literature suggestions and thematic units in it help expand students' background knowledge.

5. **Teachers adapt teaching strategies based on the individual needs of a child.** Since *Vocabulary Building Games & Activities* is designed to be used with English Language Learners, it contains many suggestions on how to adjust teaching to meet individual student needs.